Assessment Book

SOCIAL STUDIES

GROWTH OF A NATION

PEARSON

Scott Foresman

Editorial Offices: Glenview, Illinois • Parsippany, New Jersey • New York, New York
Sales Offices: Parsippany, New Jersey • Duluth, Georgia • Glenview, Illinois
Coppell, Texas • Ontario, California • Mesa, Arizona

www.sfsocialstudies.com

Program Authors

Dr. Candy Dawson Boyd
Professor, School of Education
Director of Reading Programs
St. Mary's College
Moraga, California

Dr. Geneva Gay
Professor of Education
University of Washington
Seattle, Washington

Rita Geiger
Director of Social Studies and
    Foreign Languages
Norman Public Schools
Norman, Oklahoma

Dr. James B. Kracht
Associate Dean for
    Undergraduate Programs
    and Teacher Education
College of Education
Texas A & M University
College Station, Texas

Dr. Valerie Ooka Pang
Professor of Teacher Education
San Diego State University
San Diego, California

Dr. C. Frederick Risinger
Director, Professional
    Development and Social
    Studies Education
Indiana University
Bloomington, Indiana

Sara Miranda Sanchez
Elementary and Early
    Childhood Curriculum
    Coordinator
Albuquerque Public Schools
Albuquerque, New Mexico

Contributing Authors

Dr. Carol Berkin
Professor of History
Baruch College and the
    Graduate Center
The City University of New York
New York, New York

Lee A. Chase
Staff Development Specialist
Chesterfield County
    Public Schools
Chesterfield County, Virginia

Dr. Jim Cummins
Professor of Curriculum
Ontario Institute for Studies
    in Education
University of Toronto
Toronto, Canada

Dr. Allen D. Glenn
Professor and Dean Emeritus
College of Education
Curriculum and Instruction
University of Washington
Seattle, Washington

Dr. Carole L. Hahn
Professor, Educational Studies
Emory University
Atlanta, Georgia

Dr. M. Gail Hickey
Professor of Education
Indiana University-Purdue
    University
Ft. Wayne, Indiana

Dr. Bonnie Meszaros
Associate Director
Center for Economic Education
    and Entrepreneurship
University of Delaware
Newark, Delaware

ISBN 0-328-08198-1

4 5 6 7 8 9 10-V016-12 11 10 09 08 07 06

Contents

To the Teacher

One way to evaluate the success of your social studies instruction lies in using the assessment options provided in **Scott Foresman** *Social Studies*. These options will help you measure students' progress toward social studies instructional goals.

The assessment tools provided with **Scott Foresman** *Social Studies* can

- help you determine which students need more help and where classroom instruction needs to be reinforced, reviewed, or expanded.
- help you evaluate how well students comprehend, communicate, and apply what they have learned.

Scott Foresman *Social Studies* provides a comprehensive assessment package as shown below.

Assessment Options Available in Scott Foresman *Social Studies*

Formal Assessments	Lesson Reviews, PE/TE Chapter Reviews, PE/TE Chapter Tests, Assessment Book Unit Review, PE/TE Unit Tests, Assessment Book Test Talk Practice Book ExamView® Test Bank CD-ROM
Informal Assessments	Teacher's Edition Questions Section Reviews, PE/TE Close and Assess, TE Ongoing Assessments, TE
Portfolio Assessments	Portfolio Assessments, TE Leveled Practice, TE Workbook Pages Chapter Review: Write About History, PE/TE Unit Review: Apply Skills, PE/TE Curriculum Connection: Writing, PE/TE
Performance Assessments	Hands-on Unit Project, PE/TE Internet Activity, PE Chapter Performance Assessment, TE Unit Review: Write and Share, PE/TE Scoring Guides, TE

Overview of the Assessment Book

Chapter and Unit Tests

The Chapter and Unit Tests are tools to evaluate students' understanding of critical social studies concepts and their ability to apply and analyze them. There is a four-page, reproducible test for each chapter and unit in the Student Book.

Students are asked to fill in blanks, complete sentences, choose a correct answer from a series of possible responses, draw an answer, match items, and read/complete a map, chart, or graph. There is an Answer Key for each Chapter and Unit Test at the back of the Assessment Book.

Chapter and Unit Content Tests

The two-page content test includes a series of multiple choice questions covering levels of thinking from knowledge to comprehension, application, and analysis. Each question is correlated to a student learning objective.

Chapter and Unit Skills Tests

The two-page skills test checks students' knowledge of and ability to apply the social studies skills taught in the Student Book. Each question is correlated to a specific thinking skill.

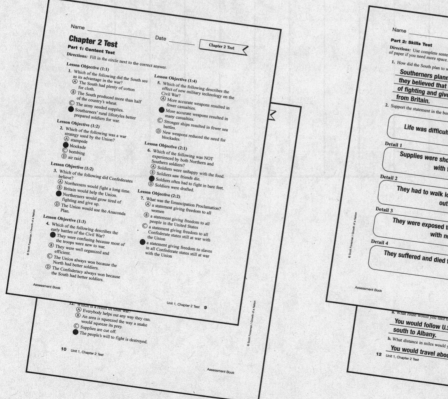

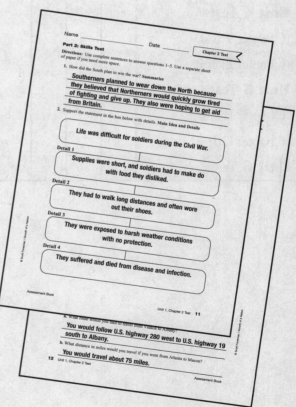

Class Record Sheet

Student Name										
Overview Unit Test										
Chapter 1 Test										
Chapter 2 Test										
Unit 1 Test										
Chapter 3 Test										
Chapter 4 Test										
Unit 2 Test										
Chapter 5 Test										
Chapter 6 Test										
Unit 3 Test										
Chapter 7 Test										
Chapter 8 Test										
Unit 4 Test										
Chapter 9 Test										
Chapter 10 Test										
Unit 5 Test										
Chapter 11 Test										
Chapter 12 Test										
Unit 6 Test										

Class Record Sheet

Student Name

Overview Unit Test										
Chapter 1 Test										
Chapter 2 Test										
Unit 1 Test										
Chapter 3 Test										
Chapter 4 Test										
Unit 2 Test										
Chapter 5 Test										
Chapter 6 Test										
Unit 3 Test										
Chapter 7 Test										
Chapter 8 Test										
Unit 4 Test										
Chapter 9 Test										
Chapter 10 Test										
Unit 5 Test										
Chapter 11 Test										
Chapter 12 Test										
Unit 6 Test										

NOTES

Overview Test

Part 1: Content Test

Directions: Fill in the circle next to the correct answer.

1. Many scholars think people first migrated to North America by
   - (A) boat.
   - (B) crossing a land bridge between Asia and North America.
   - (C) walking north from South America.
   - (D) swimming from Caribbean islands.

2. The first people to arrive in North America survived by
   - (A) hunting.
   - (B) farming.
   - (C) trading.
   - (D) manufacturing.

3. Native American cultures differed in part based on
   - (A) how long they had been living in North America.
   - (B) what part of Asia they came from.
   - (C) whether they preferred hunting or farming.
   - (D) the resources available to them.

4. Which of the following is NOT a result of the Columbian Exchange?
   - (A) Cattle and horses came from Europe to the Americas.
   - (B) Columbus landed on some islands off the coast of North America.
   - (C) Crops such as potatoes and beans came to Europe from the Americas.
   - (D) Native Americans were exposed to European diseases.

5. Which of the following is NOT one of the reasons Europeans came to the American colonies?
   - (A) religious freedom
   - (B) economic opportunity
   - (C) the chance to explore
   - (D) the absence of a fur trade

6. The Jamestown colony is remembered mainly because
   - (A) it was the first permanent English colony in North America.
   - (B) it was a major East Coast Spanish colony.
   - (C) the first Thanksgiving was held there.
   - (D) Squanto helped the Pilgrims there survive.

7. Plantations were most common in the Southern Colonies because
   - (A) most African Americans lived there.
   - (B) the soil and climate were suitable to plantation agriculture.
   - (C) southern farmers did not like growing wheat.
   - (D) the South lacked ports for a fishing industry.

8. Which of the following were NOT factors in the early colonial economy of New England?
   - (A) plentiful supply of wood
   - (B) rich fishing grounds
   - (C) warm weather for plantations
   - (D) shipping industry

9. Why were many colonists angered by the Stamp Act?
   Ⓐ They thought the tax was too high.
   Ⓑ They thought the tax was too low.
   Ⓒ They had already declared independence from Great Britain.
   Ⓓ They did not think the British government had the right to tax them.

10. Which of the following was NOT a key event of the American Revolution?
    Ⓐ Declaration of Independence
    Ⓑ Battle of Saratoga
    Ⓒ Battle of Yorktown
    Ⓓ the Constitutional Convention

11. Which of the following is NOT a key feature of the United States government under the Constitution?
    Ⓐ established by the Articles of Confederation
    Ⓑ includes checks and balances
    Ⓒ is a republic
    Ⓓ includes the Bill of Rights

12. Disagreement between members of George Washington's Cabinet helped lead the development of
    Ⓐ Washington, D.C.
    Ⓑ a strong national government.
    Ⓒ political parties.
    Ⓓ the executive branch.

13. The Louisiana Purchase
    Ⓐ belonged to Sacagawea.
    Ⓑ doubled the size of the United States.
    Ⓒ was never explored.
    Ⓓ led to war with France.

14. The great change in the way goods were manufactured that took place in the early decades of United States history is known as the
    Ⓐ Industrial Revolution.
    Ⓑ Monroe Doctrine.
    Ⓒ cotton gin.
    Ⓓ Report on Manufactures.

15. The abolitionists favored
    Ⓐ manifest destiny.
    Ⓑ war with Mexico.
    Ⓒ an end to slavery.
    Ⓓ territorial expansion of the United States.

Part 2: Skills Test

Directions: Use complete sentences to answer questions 1–5. Use a separate sheet of paper if you need more space.

1. Describe how scholars think the first humans arrived in North America and developed into different Native American groups. **Summarize**

   _____

   _____

   _____

   _____

   _____

2. What was the effect of the creation of the House of Burgesses in Virginia? **Cause and Effect**

   _____

   _____

   _____

   _____

3. What can you conclude about the abolitionists and their feelings about slavery? **Draw Conclusions**

   _____

   _____

   _____

4. Complete the chart below by summarizing the details about events in the British colonies.
Summarize

Stamp Act angers colonists.

Patriot leaders meet
in Philadelphia.

British soldiers fire on
Boston protesters.

Patriots and British fight at
Lexington and Concord.

5. Look at the map below. If you wanted to find how to drive from one city in Virginia to
another, would you seek a larger-scale map or a smaller-scale map? **Compare Maps at
Different Scales**

_____

_____

_____

_____

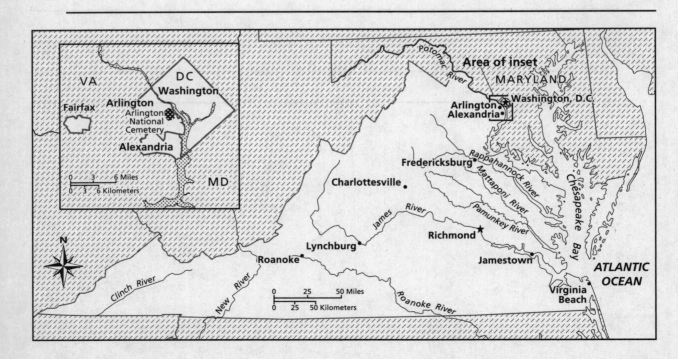

Chapter 1 Test

Part 1: Content Test

Directions: Fill in the circle next to the correct answer.

1. Where did most Southerners live by the mid-1850s?
   - Ⓐ cities and large towns
   - Ⓑ cities and plantations
   - Ⓒ farms and small towns
   - Ⓓ farms and plantations

2. In what region of the United States were most of the nation's cities located by the 1850s?
   - Ⓐ North
   - Ⓑ South
   - Ⓒ East
   - Ⓓ West

3. What was the North's point of view on slavery by the 1850s?
   - Ⓐ Most Northern states had outlawed slavery.
   - Ⓑ Most Northern states supported slavery.
   - Ⓒ Most Northern factories hired slaves for workers.
   - Ⓓ Slaves were found only on farms in the North.

4. Which of the following describes slavery's role in the Southern economy?
   - Ⓐ Slavery was expensive.
   - Ⓑ Slavery was forbidden.
   - Ⓒ Slavery was a luxury.
   - Ⓓ Slavery was profitable.

5. Which of the following is one way in which slaves resisted slavery?
   - Ⓐ telling family stories
   - Ⓑ meeting with owners
   - Ⓒ singing in the fields
   - Ⓓ holding back on work

6. Which of the following was a slave rebellion that ended in the slaves returning to Africa?
   - Ⓐ New Haven rebellion
   - Ⓑ *Amistad* rebellion
   - Ⓒ slave rebellion
   - Ⓓ abolitionists' rebellion

7. What means did Harriet Tubman and others use to help slaves reach freedom in the North?
   - Ⓐ Underground Railroad
   - Ⓑ churches
   - Ⓒ schools
   - Ⓓ *Amistad* rebellion

8. Which of the following describes the lifestyle of free African Americans?
   - Ⓐ They lived in fear of losing their freedom.
   - Ⓑ They lived the same as white citizens.
   - Ⓒ They lived as paid slaves.
   - Ⓓ They received many benefits.

9. What problem did the Missouri Compromise solve?
   (A) Southern states wanted to admit a free state.
   (B) Northerners did not want more slave states than free states.
   (C) Missouri had to choose to be a free state or a slave state.
   (D) Missouri wanted to join the United States as a free state.

10. What led to violence in Kansas in 1854?
    (A) Northerners and Southerners disagreed over the results of the slavery vote.
    (B) People voted for Kansas to be a slave state.
    (C) People voted for Kansas to be a free state.
    (D) Nebraska was split into Kansas and Nebraska.

11. Why were people outraged at the Supreme Court's decision in the Dred Scott case?
    (A) They believed it would solve many problems.
    (B) They agreed with the decision.
    (C) The Court said African Americans had no rights.
    (D) The Court ruled in favor of Scott.

12. Which statement represents Lincoln's and Douglas's views on slavery?
    (A) They agreed on slavery.
    (B) Neither one cared about slavery.
    (C) Douglas opposed slavery, but Lincoln believed slavery had its place.
    (D) Lincoln opposed slavery, but Douglas thought slavery had its place.

13. Which of the following is a reason Southern states seceded from the Union?
    (A) They wanted to support the Union.
    (B) They wanted to abolish slavery.
    (C) They wanted their own flag.
    (D) They wanted to keep slavery.

14. What officially started the Civil War?
    (A) battle at Fort Sumter
    (B) disagreements between the North and the South
    (C) disagreements between Lincoln and Davis
    (D) disagreements between abolitionists and slave owners

15. What did the North hope to achieve by fighting the Civil War?
    (A) preservation of states' rights
    (B) an end to slavery
    (C) equality for all
    (D) preservation of the slave system

Name ______________________ Date __________ **Chapter 1 Test**

Part 2: Skills Test

Directions: Use complete sentences to answer questions 1–5. Use a separate sheet of paper if you need more space.

1. Why did Southern states fear the outlawing of slavery? **Main Idea and Details**

____

____

____

____

2. In the chart below, give details that explain how the Underground Railroad was able to be so successful in its fight against slavery. **Main Idea and Details**

The Underground Railroad

3. What was the underlying issue the Missouri Compromise was intended to address? Was it successful or not? **Draw Conclusions**

____

____

____

____

____

4. Why do you think Jefferson Davis thought it was important to capture Fort Sumter? **Hypothesize**

_____

_____

_____

_____

_____

5. Complete the chart below. List some of the goals people in the United States had as they entered into the Civil War. **Main Idea and Details**

_____

_____

_____

_____

_____

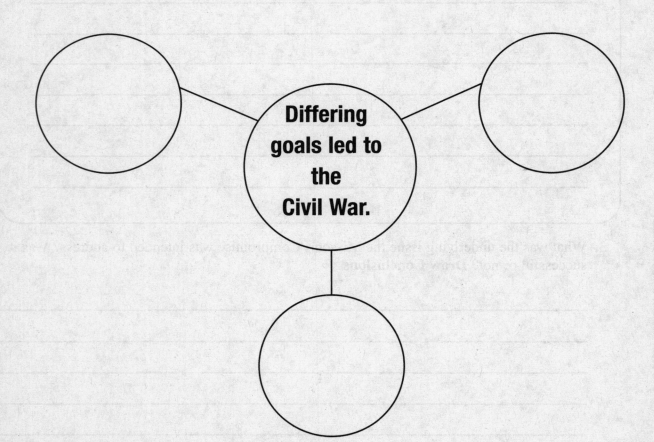

Chapter 2 Test

Part 1: Content Test

Directions: Fill in the circle next to the correct answer.

1. Which of the following did the South see as its advantage in the war?
   - Ⓐ The South had plenty of cotton for cloth.
   - Ⓑ The South produced more than half of the country's wheat.
   - Ⓒ The army needed supplies.
   - Ⓓ Southerners' rural lifestyles better prepared soldiers for war.

2. Which of the following was a war strategy used by the Union?
   - Ⓐ stampede
   - Ⓑ blockade
   - Ⓒ bombing
   - Ⓓ air raid

3. Which of the following did Confederates believe?
   - Ⓐ Northerners would fight a long time.
   - Ⓑ Britain would help the Union.
   - Ⓒ Northerners would grow tired of fighting and give up.
   - Ⓓ The Union would use the Anaconda Plan.

4. Which of the following describes the early battles of the Civil War?
   - Ⓐ They were confusing because most of the troops were new to war.
   - Ⓑ They were well organized and efficient.
   - Ⓒ The Union always won because the North had better soldiers.
   - Ⓓ The Confederacy always won because the South had better soldiers.

5. Which of the following describes the effect of new military technology on the Civil War?
   - Ⓐ More accurate weapons resulted in fewer casualties.
   - Ⓑ More accurate weapons resulted in many casualties.
   - Ⓒ Stronger ships resulted in fewer sea battles.
   - Ⓓ New weapons reduced the need for blockades.

6. Which of the following was NOT experienced by both Northern and Southern soldiers?
   - Ⓐ Soldiers were unhappy with the food.
   - Ⓑ Soldiers saw friends die.
   - Ⓒ Soldiers often had to fight in bare feet.
   - Ⓓ Soldiers were drafted.

7. What was the Emancipation Proclamation?
   - Ⓐ a statement giving freedom to all women
   - Ⓑ a statement giving freedom to all people in the United States
   - Ⓒ a statement giving freedom to all Confederate states still at war with the Union
   - Ⓓ a statement giving freedom to slaves in all Confederate states still at war with the Union

8. What is one way African Americans served the Union's war effort?
   - Ⓐ They engaged in combat.
   - Ⓑ They protested against slavery.
   - Ⓒ They supported freedom and went to Canada.
   - Ⓓ They staged demonstrations to end the war.

9. Which is NOT one way women contributed to the war effort?
   - Ⓐ They cared for the soldiers.
   - Ⓑ They ran the government.
   - Ⓒ They ran businesses.
   - Ⓓ They were spies.

10. Which of the following describes the Battle of Gettysburg?
    - Ⓐ Lee and Pickett battled against each other, and the North won.
    - Ⓑ Lee's retreat to Virginia won the battle for the South.
    - Ⓒ The Pennsylvania battle was won by the South.
    - Ⓓ The three-day struggle was won by the North.

11. Which cut the Confederacy in two?
    - Ⓐ Battle of Vicksburg
    - Ⓑ Battle of Gettysburg
    - Ⓒ Battle of Savannah
    - Ⓓ Battle of Bull Run

12. Which is a result of total war?
    - Ⓐ Everybody helps out any way they can.
    - Ⓑ An area is squeezed the way a snake would squeeze its prey.
    - Ⓒ Supplies are cut off.
    - Ⓓ The people's will to fight is destroyed.

13. Why did Congress disagree with President Andrew Johnson's Reconstruction plan?
    - Ⓐ They thought it was too easy on the South.
    - Ⓑ They did not want to include all of the Southern states.
    - Ⓒ They did not want to allow all African Americans to be free.
    - Ⓓ They thought the plan was cruel to Southerners.

14. Which of the following was an effect of the Reconstruction Acts?
    - Ⓐ All African Americans had the right to vote.
    - Ⓑ African American men had the right to vote.
    - Ⓒ African Americans could lobby Congress for the right to vote.
    - Ⓓ African Americans were not allowed to vote.

15. What did the passage of the Thirteenth, Fourteenth, and Fifteenth Amendments mean for African Americans?
    - Ⓐ African Americans were free citizens, and the men could vote.
    - Ⓑ African Americans became citizens.
    - Ⓒ Slavery was abolished.
    - Ⓓ Equal protection could not be denied any citizen.

Part 2: Skills Test

Directions: Use complete sentences to answer questions 1–5. Use a separate sheet of paper if you need more space.

1. How did the South plan to win the war? **Summarize**

   _____

   _____

   _____

   _____

2. Support the statement in the box below with details. **Main Idea and Details**

   Life was difficult for soldiers during the Civil War.

   Detail 1

   Detail 2

   Detail 3

   Detail 4

3. Why do you think General Grant allowed total war to be used to defeat Lee but then offered to feed Lee's men after their surrender? **Draw Conclusions**

_____

_____

_____

_____

4. Why did Reconstruction include the Thirteenth, Fourteenth, and Fifteenth Amendments? **Make Inferences**

_____

_____

_____

_____

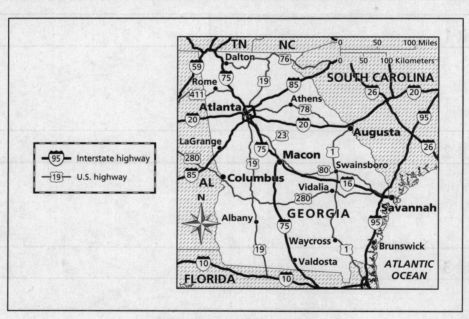

Road Map of Georgia

5. Use the map to answer the questions. **Read a Road Map**

a. What route would you take to travel from Vidalia to Albany?

_____

_____

b. What distance in miles would you travel if you went from Atlanta to Macon?

_____

Unit 1 Test

Part 1: Content Test

Directions: Fill in the circle next to the correct answer.

1. Which of the following was becoming more popular among people in the North during the 1850s?
   - Ⓐ working on small farms
   - Ⓑ working in factories
   - Ⓒ living on small farms
   - Ⓓ living in small towns

2. Why did Southerners want to preserve slavery?
   - Ⓐ Slaves were their friends.
   - Ⓑ Slaves obeyed them.
   - Ⓒ Slavery was profitable for them.
   - Ⓓ Slavery made them feel important.

3. Which of the following is a way slaves resisted slavery?
   - Ⓐ They pretended to be sick.
   - Ⓑ They held prayer meetings.
   - Ⓒ They told family stories.
   - Ⓓ They sang while they worked.

4. What was the purpose of the Underground Railroad?
   - Ⓐ It was a secret railroad that ran only at night.
   - Ⓑ It was a secret organization to turn in slaves.
   - Ⓒ It carried people to other cities at night.
   - Ⓓ It helped slaves escape to freedom.

5. What was the result of the Missouri Compromise?
   - Ⓐ Missouri would be divided into two territories.
   - Ⓑ Mississippi could be a slave state.
   - Ⓒ Missouri could choose to be a free or a slave state.
   - Ⓓ The balance was kept between free and slave states.

6. What was an effect of the Dred Scott decision?
   - Ⓐ The North and South agreed on the decision.
   - Ⓑ Many Northerners agreed with the decision.
   - Ⓒ The split between the North and the South worsened.
   - Ⓓ Most Southerners disagreed with the decision.

7. How did many Southerners feel about Lincoln's election to the presidency?
   - Ⓐ Many were happy because Lincoln was a fair man.
   - Ⓑ Many were unhappy because Lincoln was against slavery.
   - Ⓒ Many did not care because Lincoln promised to make no changes.
   - Ⓓ Many were happy because they wanted to end slavery.

8. Why did Southern states secede from the Union?
   Ⓐ Lincoln came from the North.
   Ⓑ They wanted to keep slavery.
   Ⓒ They had not voted for Lincoln.
   Ⓓ They wanted to change slavery laws.

9. What did the South hope to achieve by fighting the Civil War?
   Ⓐ preservation of slavery
   Ⓑ an end to slavery
   Ⓒ equality for all
   Ⓓ preservation of the Union

10. Which of the following was NOT an advantage held by the North during the Civil War?
    Ⓐ It produced most of the country's shoes and wheat.
    Ⓑ It had more railroads than the Confederacy.
    Ⓒ It produced more than 90 percent of the country's weapons.
    Ⓓ It had a history of producing military leaders.

11. How did new technology affect the war?
    Ⓐ Women could join the forces.
    Ⓑ Battles were less deadly.
    Ⓒ Soldiers healed more quickly.
    Ⓓ Soldiers could use weapons more accurately.

12. How did African Americans respond to the Emancipation Proclamation?
    Ⓐ Many fled to Canada.
    Ⓑ Many chose to remain slaves.
    Ⓒ Many joined the Union army.
    Ⓓ Many protested.

13. Where did Sherman use a strategy of total war to defeat the South?
    Ⓐ Georgia
    Ⓑ Pennsylvania
    Ⓒ Maryland
    Ⓓ Virginia

14. Which of the following best describes total war?
    Ⓐ Destroy all buildings and farms that might help the enemy win.
    Ⓑ Destroy all weapons.
    Ⓒ Destroy anything that might help the enemy win, including the people's will to fight.
    Ⓓ Destroy all military establishments in enemy territory.

15. Why did Congress object to Johnson's Reconstruction plan?
    Ⓐ Congress wanted stricter laws for African Americans.
    Ⓑ Congress objected to Johnson's efforts to limit African Americans' rights.
    Ⓒ Congress wanted to allow the South to do as it pleased.
    Ⓓ Congress wanted laws that were less harsh for the South.

Part 2: Skills Test

Directions: Use complete sentences to answer questions 1–5. Use a separate sheet of paper if you need more space.

1. How did lifestyles in the North and the South differ during the mid-1800s?
   Compare and Contrast

   _____

   _____

   _____

   _____

   _____

2. What do you think were two long-term effects of the Dred Scott decision? **Draw Conclusions**

   _____

   _____

   _____

   _____

3. What steps led to the outbreak of the Civil War? **Sequence**

   _____

   _____

   _____

   _____

4. Complete the chart below. Support the main idea in the box with details.
   Main Idea and Details

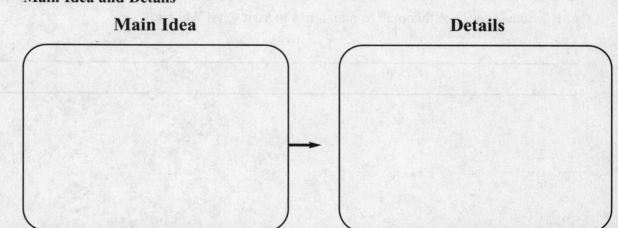

Main Idea		**Details**

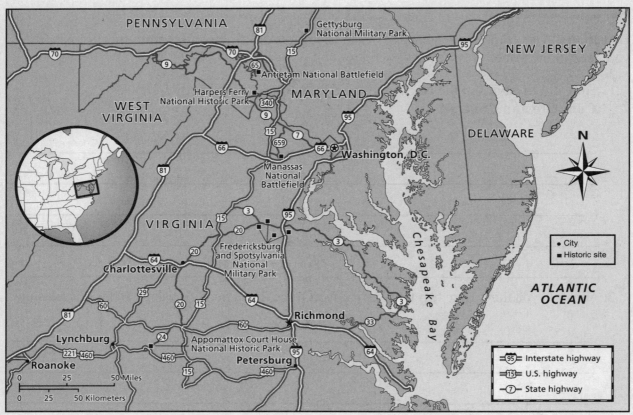

Road Map of Maryland and Eastern Virginia

5. Use the map to answer the questions. **Read a Road Map**
   a. What interstate highway would you use to travel from Charlottesville to Richmond?

   _____

   b. How many miles along interstate highway 95 would you travel going from Richmond to Petersburg?

   _____

   c. How could you use this map to plan a trip to visit Civil War sites?

   _____

   _____

Chapter 3 Test

Part 1: Content Test

Directions: Fill in the circle next to the correct answer.

1. Which innovation used electricity to send news across the country?
   - Ⓐ the transcontinental railroad
   - Ⓑ the Pony Express
   - Ⓒ the telegraph
   - Ⓓ the stagecoach

2. Which of the following best describes a major challenge faced by the Union Pacific railroad?
   - Ⓐ conflict with Native Americans
   - Ⓑ conflict with Chinese immigrants
   - Ⓒ competition among other railroad companies
   - Ⓓ the steep slopes of the Sierra Nevada

3. Which group made up the largest part of the Central Pacific's workforce?
   - Ⓐ Irish immigrants
   - Ⓑ Chinese immigrants
   - Ⓒ African Americans
   - Ⓓ former Union Army soldiers

4. Which innovation allowed people and goods to travel across the country in just a week?
   - Ⓐ the stagecoach
   - Ⓑ the Pony Express
   - Ⓒ the transcontinental railroad
   - Ⓓ the Morse Code

5. What was the main purpose of the Homestead Act?
   - Ⓐ to bring an end to cattle drives
   - Ⓑ to encourage settlement on the Great Plains
   - Ⓒ to defeat the Native Americans
   - Ⓓ to provide a market for steel plows

6. Which of the following was NOT one of the challenges typically faced by homesteaders?
   - Ⓐ high cost of land
   - Ⓑ harsh weather
   - Ⓒ large amount of grasshoppers
   - Ⓓ thick sod

7. Why did many exodusters come to the Great Plains?
   - Ⓐ European immigrants forced them from their homes in the East.
   - Ⓑ They wanted to hunt buffalo.
   - Ⓒ They faced discrimination and lack of opportunity in the East.
   - Ⓓ They were seeking religious freedom.

8. Which of the following was NOT a way that technology helped pioneers turn the Great Plains into productive farmland?
   - Ⓐ Stronger steel plows were used on the thick grasslands.
   - Ⓑ Windmills were used to pump water to the land's surface.
   - Ⓒ Barbed wire was used to keep animals away from crops.
   - Ⓓ Sod was used as a building material to keep out bugs.

9. Why were cattle drives profitable for Texas ranchers?
   (A) Cattle grew fatter as they traveled the trails.
   (B) People paid to watch the cattle drives.
   (C) Cattle could be sold for more money in the East.
   (D) Railroads paid ranchers to use their services.

10. Which of the following best describes a reason why cattle drives came to an end?
   (A) Thousands of cattle ranchers moved west in search of gold.
   (B) Consumers became more interested in gold than cattle.
   (C) Farmers on the Great Plains began raising cattle.
   (D) They were no longer necessary once railroads reached Texas.

11. Which of the following describes a lasting effect of the search for gold?
   (A) The quest for gold lured many settlers to the West.
   (B) Gold rushes left the West deserted with ghost towns.
   (C) Dreams of finding gold continue to attract many settlers each year.
   (D) Few miners actually found gold nuggets.

12. Which of the following was NOT a change that threatened the way of life for Native Americans of the Great Plains?
   (A) decline in buffalo herds
   (B) widespread European diseases
   (C) spreading telegraph and railroad lines
   (D) arrival of miners, farmers, and ranchers

13. Why is the Battle of Little Bighorn also known as "Custer's Last Stand"?
   (A) Custer resigned after witnessing the brutal Lakota defeat.
   (B) Custer was seriously injured as he led his forces to victory.
   (C) Custer was killed along with his entire forces.
   (D) Custer surrendered after his forces were surrounded by the Lakota.

14. Which of the following describes the significance of the Battle of Wounded Knee?
   (A) It was the biggest victory Native Americans ever won over United States forces.
   (B) It was the last major battle between the United States and Native Americans.
   (C) It convinced the United States government to take stronger action against the Lakota and other Native American groups.
   (D) It allowed Native Americans to return to their traditional homelands.

15. Which of the following is NOT an example of how Native American groups are keeping traditions alive today?
   (A) gaining control of more land
   (B) maintaining tribal languages
   (C) sharing tribal stories
   (D) launching raids on United States military sites

Part 2: Skills Test

Directions: Use complete sentences to answer questions 1–5. Use a separate sheet of paper if you need more space.

1. Write the following events about transportation and communication in the order in which they happened. **Sequence**

The first telegraph line across the country was completed.

A new business called the Pony Express began delivering mail from Missouri to California in just 10 days.

The tracks of the Union Pacific and Central Pacific met at Promontory Point, Utah.

Samuel Morse developed a method of sending messages along wires.

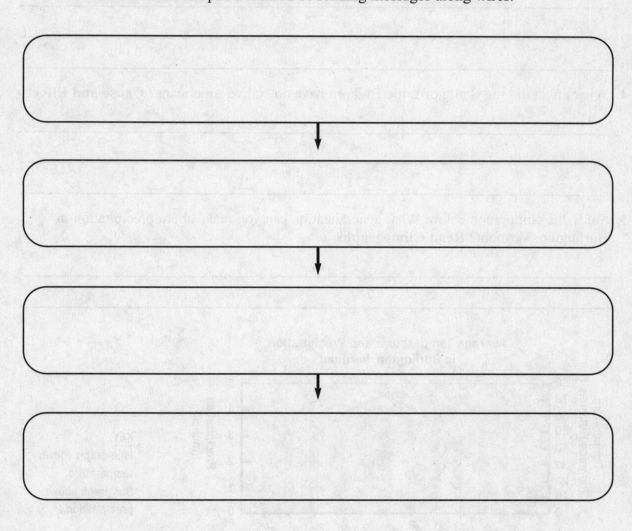

2. Use details from the chapter to support the following statement. **Main Idea and Details**

Gold rushes of the mid-1800s had lasting effects in the West.

_____

_____

_____

_____

3. What can you infer from the fact that the United States government forced many Native Americans of the Great Plains to move to reservations in the late 1800s? **Make Inferences**

_____

_____

_____

4. What effect did the Battle of Little Bighorn have on Native Americans? **Cause and Effect**

_____

_____

_____

5. Study the climograph below. What generalization can you make about precipitation in Burlington, Vermont? **Read Climographs**

_____

_____

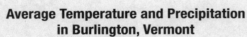

Average Temperature and Precipitation in Burlington, Vermont

KEY
Line graph shows temperature.
Bar graph shows precipitation.

Chapter 4 Test

Part 1: Content Test

Directions: Fill in the circle next to the correct answer.

1. Who invented the telephone?
   Ⓐ Alexander Graham Bell
   Ⓑ Lewis Latimer
   Ⓒ Frank Sprague
   Ⓓ Frank Duryea

2. Which of the following did Thomas Edison invent?
   Ⓐ the airplane
   Ⓑ the electric streetcar
   Ⓒ the phonograph
   Ⓓ the gasoline engine

3. Which of the following represents an invention that changed transportation at the turn of the twentieth century?
   Ⓐ the wagon
   Ⓑ the Pony Express
   Ⓒ the electric streetcar
   Ⓓ the stagecoach

4. Which of the following is NOT an example of how inventions of the late 1800s and early 1900s led to the rise of new industries?
   Ⓐ Companies all over the country began selling and designing cars.
   Ⓑ People started businesses to offer telephone service.
   Ⓒ Airplane manufacturing became the country's leading industry.
   Ⓓ Entrepreneurs built power stations to bring electricity to cities.

5. Andrew Carnegie is known for which of the following?
   Ⓐ inventing a new method for making steel
   Ⓑ building a huge steel empire
   Ⓒ building oil refineries
   Ⓓ forming the Westinghouse Electric Company

6. Which business leader founded Standard Oil Company?
   Ⓐ Edwin Drake
   Ⓑ John D. Rockefeller
   Ⓒ William Randolph Hearst
   Ⓓ Madame C. J. Walker

7. Which of the following best describes how railroads helped the United States economy grow?
   Ⓐ They charged high rates to farmers.
   Ⓑ They used many tons of steel.
   Ⓒ They helped end the shipping industry.
   Ⓓ They helped businesses reach distant markets.

8. Which of the following describes a free enterprise system?
   (A) Consumers have few choices about where they can buy goods and services.
   (B) Competition rarely exists among business owners.
   (C) The government regulates what business owners can produce and how much they can charge for products and services.
   (D) Business owners can decide what to produce and how much to charge for products or services.

9. The growth of big business led to all EXCEPT which of the following?
   (A) By 1900, more Americans worked in factories than on farms.
   (B) People moved by the millions to rural areas.
   (C) Big business created millions of jobs.
   (D) The United States became the world's leading producer of manufactured goods.

10. Which of the following is one of the main reasons immigrants came to the United States in the late 1800s and early 1900s?
    (A) They did not want religious freedom.
    (B) They hoped for economic opportunity.
    (C) They faced a lack of prejudice.
    (D) They wanted to live more simply.

11. Angel Island differed from Ellis Island in that
    (A) it was the main immigrant station for European immigrants.
    (B) it was the main immigrant station for Chinese immigrants.
    (C) Angel Island was located on the East Coast.
    (D) most people stopped there for only a few hours.

12. Immigrants often lived in communities with others from their home country because
    (A) it was illegal for them to live elsewhere.
    (B) they had no interest in building new lives in the United States.
    (C) it was a way to help make the adjustment to the United States easier.
    (D) housing was not available in other areas.

13. Which of the following was NOT a contributing factor that led to the rise of labor unions?
    (A) Many workers earned low wages and worked long hours.
    (B) Many business owners were going on strike.
    (C) Working conditions were often unhealthy and dangerous.
    (D) Many workers labored in hot, cramped workshops.

14. Which of the following was NOT a main goal of the American Federation of Labor?
Ⓐ safer working conditions
Ⓑ end child labor
Ⓒ better wages
Ⓓ a 12-hour workday

15. Which of the following events shows how conditions improved for workers in the early 1900s?
Ⓐ the Homestead strike
Ⓑ the Triangle Shirtwaist fire
Ⓒ the completion of the transcontinental railroad
Ⓓ the establishment of Labor Day

Part 2: Skills Test

Directions: Use complete sentences to answer questions 1–5. Use a separate sheet of paper if you need more space.

1. Write the following events in the order in which they happened. **Sequence**

Lewis Latimer developed a method that made electric light practical for every day use.

Thomas Edison built an electric power station in New York City.

Frank Sprague designed the world's first system of electric streetcars.

Thomas Edison built a light bulb that glowed for two days.

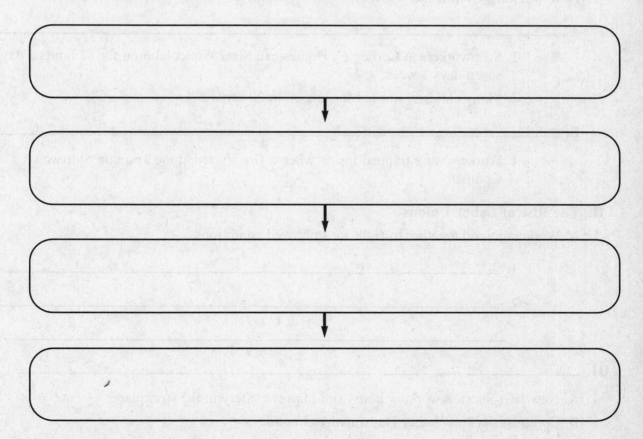

2. Why do monopolies threaten the free enterprise system? **Draw Conclusions**

_____

_____

_____

3. How did the growth of the automobile industry effect the oil industry? **Cause and Effect**

_____

_____

4. What challenges did many immigrants face once they gained entry into the United States? **Main Idea and Details**

_____

_____

5. Complete the outline by filling in the missing topics and details about the labor movement. **Write an Outline**

The Labor Movement

I. Poor working Conditions

   A. _____

      1. Steelworkers at Carnegie's Homestead Steel Works labored for 12 hours a day, seven days a week.

      2. Many children worked for just 10 to 20 cents a day.

   B. _____

      1. Workers were trapped inside when a fire started at the Triangle Shirtwaist Company.

II. The Rise of Labor Unions

   A. Workers joined together to fight for improved conditions.

      1. _____

      2. _____

         _____

III. _____

   A. New laws shorten working hours and improve safety in the workplace.

   B. Congress declares Labor Day a national holiday.

Unit 2 Test

Part 1: Content Test

Directions: Fill in the circle next to the correct answer.

1. Which of the following could deliver mail from Missouri to California in just 10 days?
   - Ⓐ the telegraph
   - Ⓑ the "horseless carriage"
   - Ⓒ the Pony Express
   - Ⓓ the stagecoach

2. Which of the following describes a challenge faced by the Union Pacific railroad?
   - Ⓐ It had to build through the Sierra Nevada.
   - Ⓑ It faced conflict with Native Americans.
   - Ⓒ It faced conflict with Chinese immigrants.
   - Ⓓ The government did not support a transcontinental railroad.

3. Which best describes a challenge facing homesteaders on the Great Plains?
   - Ⓐ They had to pay about $10 for 160 acres of land.
   - Ⓑ Land on the Great Plains was dry but very fertile.
   - Ⓒ They had to pass through miles of barbed wire.
   - Ⓓ They had to bust through sod before planting crops.

4. Steel plows were especially important to Great Plains farmers because
   - Ⓐ there was a shortage of iron.
   - Ⓑ there was a shortage of farm animals to pull plows.
   - Ⓒ the sod was extremely thick on the Great Plains.
   - Ⓓ steel plows were less costly than iron ones.

5. The arrival of railroads in Texas helped end the cattle drives because
   - Ⓐ they made it unnecessary to drive cattle to distant railroad centers.
   - Ⓑ the railroads blocked key cattle trails.
   - Ⓒ easterners could come to Texas to buy meat.
   - Ⓓ buffalo replaced cattle as a major meat source.

6. Which of the following was NOT an effect of the search for gold in the West?
   - Ⓐ Supply stations for miners grew into important cities.
   - Ⓑ Gold rushes left the East deserted with ghost towns.
   - Ⓒ Dreams of finding gold attracted thousands of settlers.
   - Ⓓ Growing towns offered opportunities for entrepreneurs.

7. The Battle of Little Bighorn convinced the United States that

Ⓐ it would not be able to defeat certain Native American groups.

Ⓑ the conflict would not be resolved until Native Americans could return to their traditional homelands.

Ⓒ moving Native American groups to reservations was not a good idea.

Ⓓ it should take stronger action against Native Americans.

8. Which of the following did Thomas Edison invent?

Ⓐ a light bulb with a carbon filament

Ⓑ the typewriter

Ⓒ the radio

Ⓓ the automobile

9. What do the electric street car and the "horseless carriage" have in common?

Ⓐ They were invented by Thomas Edison.

Ⓑ They were both outlawed at one time.

Ⓒ They changed transportation at the turn of the twentieth century.

Ⓓ They were outdated by the early 1900s.

10. George Westinghouse is known for

Ⓐ his monopoly of the oil industry.

Ⓑ developing a new technology for delivering electricity.

Ⓒ controlling the banking industry.

Ⓓ building a steel empire.

11. Which of the following is a result of the rise of big business in the late 1800s and early 1900s?

Ⓐ More people left the United States to live in other countries.

Ⓑ Many people moved from cities to rural areas.

Ⓒ The United States became the world's biggest producer of manufactured goods.

Ⓓ Many United States cities became ghost towns.

12. Which of the following is NOT a reason why many immigrants came to the United States in the late 1800s and early 1900s?

Ⓐ to escape poverty

Ⓑ to escape hunger

Ⓒ they had many rights at home

Ⓓ they faced a lack of religious freedom at home

13. What did Ellis Island and Angel Island share in common?

Ⓐ Both were located on the West Coast.

Ⓑ Both were located on the East Coast.

Ⓒ Both held immigrants until they could prove they had relatives living in the country.

Ⓓ Both were main immigration stations for immigrants arriving in the country.

14. Which of the following describes the typical week of a steelworker at Carnegie's Homestead Steel Works?
  - Ⓐ five days a week, eight hours a day
  - Ⓑ five days a week, ten hours a day
  - Ⓒ seven days a week, four hours a day
  - Ⓓ seven days a week, twelve hours a day

15. Which of the following best describes the main goals of labor unions such as the American Federation of Labor?
  - Ⓐ to get higher pay, shorter working hours, and safer working conditions
  - Ⓑ to hire new workers and start new holidays
  - Ⓒ to organize strikes and find new jobs
  - Ⓓ to pass child labor laws

Part 2: Skills Test

Directions: Use complete sentences to answer questions 1–5. Use a separate sheet of paper if you need more space.

1. Describe the changes that took place in transportation in the late 1800s.
Main Idea and Details

_____

_____

_____

_____

_____

2. What was the purpose of the Homestead Act? **Summarize**

_____

_____

3. What conditions led to the rise of labor unions in the late 1800s and early 1900s?
Cause and Effect

_____

_____

_____

_____

4. Write the following events in the order in which they happened. **Sequence**

Crazy Horse led the Lakota to victory at the Battle of Little Bighorn.

Gold was discovered in the Black Hills.

The Lakota signed a treaty with the United States that created the Great Lakota Reservation.

5. Look at the map below. What time is it in Boston when it is 4:00 P.M. in Los Angeles?
Read a Time Zone Map

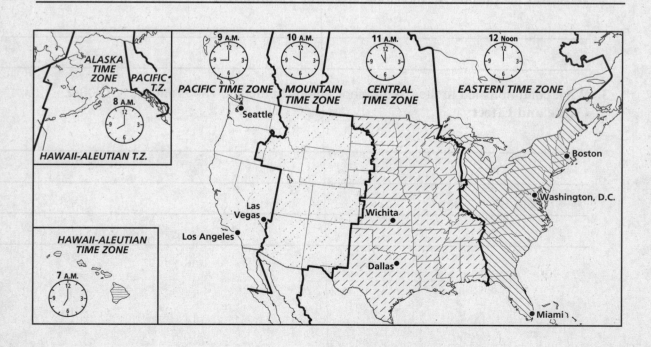

Chapter 5 Test

Part 1: Content Test

Directions: Fill in the circle next to the correct answer.

1. How did the mechanization of farms change the lives of rural people in the 1800s and early 1900s?
   - Ⓐ It led them to grow fewer crops.
   - Ⓑ It increased the need for farm labor.
   - Ⓒ It forced farmers into deeper and deeper debt.
   - Ⓓ It led to larger farms that raised cash crops.

2. Which is NOT an example of how industry in the late 1880s gave people greater access to all kinds of goods?
   - Ⓐ More goods were being invented and produced.
   - Ⓑ People on farms and ranches made almost everything they needed by hand.
   - Ⓒ Goods were less expensive to buy than ever before.
   - Ⓓ Stores increased in number, and mail-order businesses were established.

3. In what way did telephones affect life in the 1800s?
   - Ⓐ People were pleased to be able to communicate without having to travel.
   - Ⓑ Most people no longer wanted or needed to use the mail system.
   - Ⓒ Alexander Graham Bell's company filled rural areas with telephone poles.
   - Ⓓ People protested against the sight of poles and lines.

4. What was the main purpose of the Rural Electrification Act?
   - Ⓐ to encourage the use of wind and water power
   - Ⓑ to create streetcar systems in cities
   - Ⓒ to create and improve electric service in rural areas
   - Ⓓ to end people's need for electricity

5. Which of the following was NOT a factor in the growth of cities in the late 1800s?
   - Ⓐ agricultural depression
   - Ⓑ mechanization of farms
   - Ⓒ immigration
   - Ⓓ urbanization

6. What was one result of rapid industrialization and urbanization?
   - Ⓐ Most people in cities started living in large homes.
   - Ⓑ Factories moved away from residential areas.
   - Ⓒ People quit their city jobs and moved to the country.
   - Ⓓ Cities became overcrowded.

7. Which is NOT one of the challenges faced by urban areas as a result of population and technological changes?
   - Ⓐ There was more garbage and waste.
   - Ⓑ The air became polluted.
   - Ⓒ Fewer workers were available for factory jobs.
   - Ⓓ Diseases spread quickly among people living close together.

8. How did Jane Addams try to solve some of the problems faced by the city of Chicago?

Ⓐ She started schools for under-privileged city children.

Ⓑ She opened a settlement house to help immigrants and working families.

Ⓒ She wrote articles for the *New York Tribune* about the hardships faced by immigrants.

Ⓓ She was active in the YMCA.

9. What is one thing that African Americans, Hispanic groups, Chinese immigrants, and Jews had in common in the late 1800s?

Ⓐ Many faced prejudice and segregation in different areas of their lives.

Ⓑ They ran for public office in great numbers and quickly gained political power.

Ⓒ Most moved away from cities to work on farms.

Ⓓ Many became leaders in the manufacturing industry and earned a great deal of money.

10. What effect did the passage of Jim Crow laws in the 1880s have on the lives of African Americans?

Ⓐ It made racial segregation illegal in the United States.

Ⓑ It made racial segregation legal in the South.

Ⓒ It made better jobs available to African Americans.

Ⓓ It improved education for African American schoolchildren.

11. Which of the following was NOT a factor in the Great Migration?

Ⓐ World War I

Ⓑ northern African American newspapers

Ⓒ encouragement of northern African Americans

Ⓓ total equality for African Americans in the North

12. How did African American activist Booker T. Washington respond to discrimination and work toward equality?

Ⓐ He started an African American newspaper.

Ⓑ He became a scientist.

Ⓒ He founded the Tuskegee Institute, a college for African Americans.

Ⓓ He helped start the National Association for the Advancement of Colored People.

13. What happened as a result of the women's suffrage movement?

Ⓐ Women were no longer allowed to do certain jobs in factories or on farms.

Ⓑ Congress passed the Nineteenth Amendment, which gave women the right to vote.

Ⓒ Women were allowed to enter the armed services.

Ⓓ New inventions made housework and farm work easier to do.

14. Which is NOT an example of the new rights and educational opportunities gained for women in the 1800s?

Ⓐ Women could work on farms.

Ⓑ Women earned the right to vote.

Ⓒ Some colleges opened their doors to women.

Ⓓ A woman was elected mayor of a town.

15. For what is Susan B. Anthony most famous?

Ⓐ working as a spy during World War I

Ⓑ climbing mountains all over the world

Ⓒ becoming the first woman mayor in the United States

Ⓓ working for women's suffrage

Part 2: Skills Test

Directions: Use complete sentences to answer questions 1–5. Use a separate sheet of paper if you need more space.

1. Complete the chart below. Compare and contrast Booker T. Washington and W. E. B. Du Bois. **Compare and Contrast**

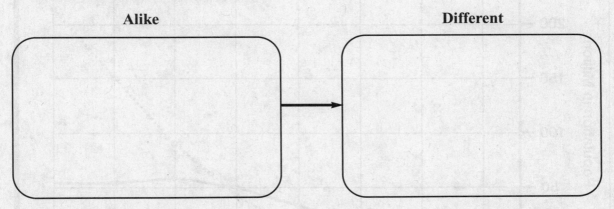

Alike

Different

2. Explain how sharecropping often led to a life of poverty and debt. **Cause and Effect**

_____

_____

_____

_____

3. How did the roles of women in the 1800s differ depending on whether they lived in rural or urban areas? **Summarize**

_____

_____

_____

4. What can you conclude from the fact that many African Americans in the South did not accept the idea of "separate but equal"? **Draw Conclusions**

_____

_____

5. Look at the graph below. In which year did the urban population first become greater than the rural population? **Read a Line Graph**

_____

_____

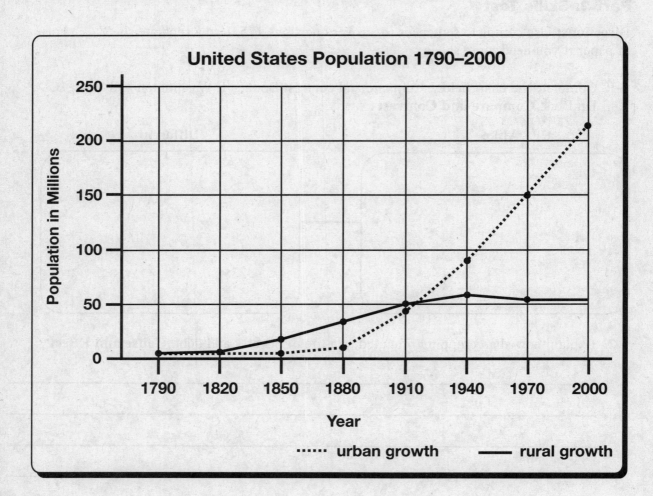

United States Population 1790–2000

Population in Millions

250
200
150
100
50
0

1790 1820 1850 1880 1910 1940 1970 2000

Year

······ urban growth   ——— rural growth

Chapter 6 Test

Part 1: Content Test

Directions: Fill in the circle next to the correct answer.

1. Which of the following did NOT come under United States control in the late 1800s?
   - Ⓐ Puerto Rico
   - Ⓑ Alaska
   - Ⓒ Cuba
   - Ⓓ Hawaii

2. What eventually drew settlers to areas of Alaska?
   - Ⓐ large cities
   - Ⓑ war
   - Ⓒ gold
   - Ⓓ farmland

3. Yellow journalism helped contribute to the start of the Spanish-American War by
   - Ⓐ inflaming public opinion in the United States against Spain.
   - Ⓑ providing an accurate and thorough record of events in Cuba.
   - Ⓒ uncovering the truth about what happened to the *Maine*.
   - Ⓓ forcing the Spanish to negotiate.

4. Which of the following was NOT a result of the Spanish-American War?
   - Ⓐ The United States was no longer viewed as a powerful nation.
   - Ⓑ Theodore Roosevelt became a national hero.
   - Ⓒ The United States gained control of Puerto Rico, the Philippines, and Guam.
   - Ⓓ The United States proved that it was a powerful nation.

5. Which of the following is NOT a reform that occurred during the Roosevelt presidency?
   - Ⓐ the Meat Inspection Act
   - Ⓑ the end of income tax
   - Ⓒ the Pure Food and Drug Act
   - Ⓓ improvement of education for children

6. Why was Roosevelt convinced that he must break up trusts?
   - Ⓐ Trusts weren't making enough money.
   - Ⓑ He was afraid of Progressives.
   - Ⓒ He felt leaders of trusts would eventually drive him from office.
   - Ⓓ Trusts were driving out competition and charging unfair prices.

7. Who is the muckraker who wrote a series of articles about the dangers of trusts?
   - Ⓐ John Muir
   - Ⓑ Upton Sinclair
   - Ⓒ Ida Tarbell
   - Ⓓ Theodore Roosevelt

8. With what is Progressive Upton Sinclair credited?
   - Ⓐ writing a novel called *The Jungle* that told about conditions in the meatpacking plants of Chicago
   - Ⓑ signing various reform acts and speaking out against trusts
   - Ⓒ writing a series of articles about coal mining
   - Ⓓ creating Blue Laws

9. Which of the following is NOT one of the ways in which the Progressive Movement changed workplaces?
  Ⓐ Coal mines were inspected.
  Ⓑ Building codes made factories safer.
  Ⓒ Young children were kept from working in factories.
  Ⓓ Children could work in factories as long as they attended school.

10. Which of the following was NOT one of the accomplishments of Progressives?
  Ⓐ income tax
  Ⓑ larger companies
  Ⓒ Blue Laws
  Ⓓ building codes

11. Which of the following was NOT one of the factors that helped set the stage for the outbreak of World War I?
  Ⓐ growing nationalism in Europe
  Ⓑ competition between the nations of Europe
  Ⓒ alliances among different nations of Europe
  Ⓓ isolationism among the nations of Europe

12. During World War I, what did the countries of Great Britain, France, Russia, Serbia, and Belgium become known as?
  Ⓐ the Central Alliance
  Ⓑ the Allied Powers
  Ⓒ the Central Powers
  Ⓓ the European Alliance

13. Which is NOT one of the reasons why the United States decided to break its policy of isolationism and enter World War I?
  Ⓐ A German submarine sank the British steamship *Lusitania* and killed more than 100 U.S. citizens.
  Ⓑ Germany promised to help Mexico get back lands it had lost to the United States.
  Ⓒ Immigrants in the United States were born in some of the countries that were fighting the war.
  Ⓓ German submarines sank three American-owned trade ships.

14. What is one example of the way in which new technologies in World War I changed the way battles were fought?
  Ⓐ Soldiers dug trenches.
  Ⓑ Soldiers traveled by sea.
  Ⓒ Guns were used regularly in battle.
  Ⓓ Airplanes became a weapon of war.

15. Which is NOT a true statement about the impact of World War I in the United States?
  Ⓐ Some women went to work in factories to take over jobs men had done.
  Ⓑ Most Americans argued against the war and refused to support the war effort in any way.
  Ⓒ The government set up a Food Administration to encourage people to eat less and send food to soldiers.
  Ⓓ People started growing food in "war gardens" to send to soldiers fighting overseas.

Part 2: Skills Test

Directions: Use complete sentences to answer questions 1–5. Use a separate sheet of paper if you need more space.

1. What was the effect of the Spanish-American War on the United States and its place in the world? **Cause and Effect**

   _____

   _____

2. Summarize the actions of the United States throughout World War I. **Summarize**

   _____

   _____

   _____

   _____

3. Complete the chart below. Compare and contrast the U.S. acquisition of Hawaii and Alaska. **Compare and Contrast**

   Alike | **Different**

4. Suppose you are living in the United States during the Theodore Roosevelt era. You don't know much about the activities of the Progressives and want to gather background information about them. Which of the following sources is probably most credible for this purpose? For what might the other sources be useful? Explain your reasoning on the lines that follow. **Credibility of a Source**

A piece by the owner of a large company that must now follow new rules.

A news article by a reporter who is looking at only facts.

A letter by a factory worker whose work conditions have improved as a result of the Progressives.

_____

_____

_____

_____

_____

_____

5. What is a political cartoon? Write your answer on the lines provided. Then, in the space below, draw a political cartoon that tries to get people thinking about the problems of industrial society in the early 1900s. Think about what details you might include in your cartoon in order to make your point. **Interpret Political Cartoons**

_____

_____

_____

Unit 3 Test

Part 1: Content Test

Directions: Fill in the circle next to the correct answer.

1. In general, how did the spread of farm mechanization affect the size of farms in the United States?
   A It made them larger.
   B It made them smaller.
   C It had no effect.
   D It made some smaller and some larger.

2. How did manufacturers help make it possible for rural residents to acquire manufactured goods?
   A They sent out salespeople.
   B They organized regular bus trips to urban shopping districts.
   C They developed mail-order catalogs.
   D They installed telephones.

3. Which of the following was a major factor in causing urban populations to grow in the United States in the late 1800s and early 1900s?
   A war with Spain
   B Progressive reforms
   C rural depression
   D immigration

4. Which was a result of population and technological changes in urban areas in the late 1800s?
   A There was less pollution.
   B There was more garbage, waste, and disease.
   C There were too few workers.
   D People moved away from cities.

5. In the late 1800s and early 1900s, racial segregation
   A had largely been wiped out in the United States.
   B affected only African Americans.
   C affected a number of minority groups, including the Chinese and African Americans.
   D was declared unconstitutional by the Supreme Court.

6. Which answer most closely represents what African Americans found in the North during the Great Migration?
   A many jobs and much fairer treatment
   B no jobs but social equality
   C much worse conditions than they had faced in the South
   D better job opportunities but continued discrimination and segregation

7. What was the main purpose of the women's suffrage movement?
   A to get women elected to Congress
   B to get voting rights for women
   C to get people to take inventions by women seriously
   D to get women the right to work on farms

8. In general, women had their earliest success in winning voting rights in rural areas of the West because
   (A) few men lived there.
   (B) more African Americans lived in these areas than urban areas.
   (C) few immigrants lived in rural areas.
   (D) women enjoyed more overall equality in these areas.

9. This was considered to be a useless, frozen wasteland until gold was discovered there in the late 1800s.
   (A) Alaska
   (B) Hawaii
   (C) Guam
   (D) Cuba

10. Theodore Roosevelt emerged from the Spanish-American War as
    (A) a wounded soldier.
    (B) a national hero.
    (C) President of the United States.
    (D) an honorary Buffalo Soldier.

11. Which of the following is a reform that occurred during the Roosevelt presidency?
    (A) less powerful laws for companies that produce food
    (B) the breakup of trusts
    (C) the end of income tax
    (D) the strengthening of oil companies

12. With what is Progressive Ida Tarbell credited?
    (A) writing a series of articles about the dangers of trusts
    (B) creating Blue Laws
    (C) changing child labor laws
    (D) writing a novel about dangerous practices in the meatpacking industry

13. Which of the following was NOT considered an achievement of the Progressives?
    (A) Blue Laws
    (B) breaking up of trusts
    (C) laws to ensure pure food and medicine
    (D) building the Panama Canal

14. Which of the following countries was NOT a member of the Allied Powers?
    (A) Germany
    (B) Great Britain
    (C) Serbia
    (D) Russia

15. When United States troops entered World War I, what effect did they have on the war?
    (A) The Central Powers became energized.
    (B) There was more trench warfare.
    (C) The Allied Powers quickly gained a military advantage.
    (D) The Germans decided to use poison gas for the first time.

Part 2: Skills Test

Directions: Use complete sentences to answer questions 1–5. Use a separate sheet of paper if you need more space.

1. If you wanted to show how the entire United States population was divided into different racial groups, which would be better: a line graph or a circle graph? Explain your answer. **Compare Line and Circle Graphs**

   _____

   _____

   _____

   _____

2. Complete the chart below. Compare and contrast the role of women of the 1800s before and after industrialization. What changed? What stayed the same? **Compare and Contrast**

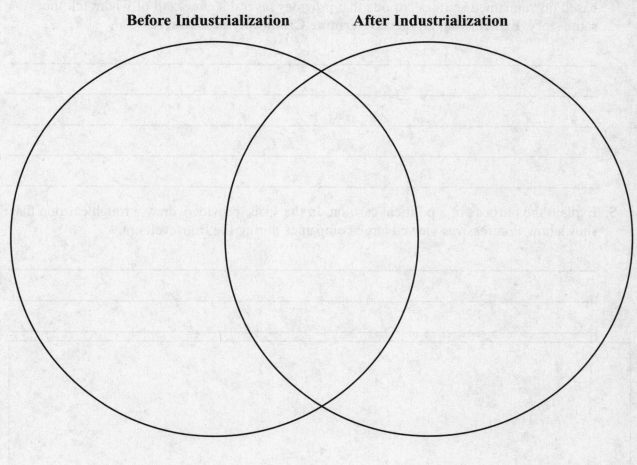

Before Industrialization   **After Industrialization**

3. Write the following events in the order in which they took place. **Sequence**

The Panama Canal is built.

Spain is defeated.

Hawaii is annexed.

Theodore Roosevelt becomes President.

Alaska is purchased.

_____

_____

_____

4. Which of the following is most likely the more credible source: A newspaper story that is based on "unnamed sources" or one that provides several sources, all of whom tell the same story. Explain your answer. **Determine Credibility of a Source**

_____

_____

_____

_____

_____

5. Explain the purpose of a political cartoon. In the space provided, draw a rough cartoon that shows how Progressives viewed large companies during the Roosevelt era.

_____

_____

_____

Chapter 7 Test

Part 1: Content Test

Directions: Fill in the circle next to the correct answer.

1. What allowed Henry Ford's Model Ts to be sold for less than half the cost of other cars?
   A the use of cheaper materials
   B the use of an assembly line
   C not following safety standards
   D the fact that no two cars were exactly alike

2. Which of the following is NOT a way in which the automobile changed life in the United States?
   A Farmers had to carry their crops to market.
   B Roads were improved.
   C It created many new jobs.
   D People moved farther from their jobs.

3. Why were romantic dramas nicknamed "soap operas"?
   A Most people watched them at the laundromat.
   B They encouraged people to go to the opera.
   C They were often paid for by opera companies.
   D They were often paid for by soap companies.

4. Which of the following describes a reason why Prohibition failed?
   A Police had little success in stopping bootleggers.
   B Many bootleggers moved their businesses to Canada.
   C Many people moved to Europe, where they could still buy alcohol.
   D Many people spent their money on their families instead of on alcohol.

5. Which musician recorded "St. Louis Blues" with Bessie Smith?
   A Duke Ellington
   B Louis Armstrong
   C George Gershwin
   D Aaron Copland

6. Which Harlem Renaissance figure created several series of paintings that showed African American life and history?
   A Jacob Lawrence
   B Langston Hughes
   C Zora Neale Hurston
   D James Weldon Johnson

7. How did mass media help make athletes popular in the 1920s?
   A Most movies were about sports.
   B Many newspaper articles were paid for by sports teams.
   C Many athletes starred in radio dramas.
   D Radio made it possible for fans to listen to sports games.

8. How did working life change for women in the 1920s?
   - (A) A greater percentage of women joined the workforce.
   - (B) Many women moved from farming to manufacturing.
   - (C) Many women moved from factory work to office jobs.
   - (D) Many women earned the same wages as men.

9. Which of the following describes the economy in the 1920s?
   - (A) The mining industry grew as coal replaced oil for fuel.
   - (B) The lumber industry grew as builders began using wood instead of concrete.
   - (C) Crop prices fell and many farmers had difficulty paying off debts.
   - (D) Factory workers were unable to produce enough goods.

10. Which of the following describes what happened during the stock market crash of 1929?
    - (A) Stock prices fell and many investors sold their stocks.
    - (B) Stock prices rose and many investors sold their stocks.
    - (C) Stock prices fell and many investors purchased stocks.
    - (D) Stock prices rose and many investors purchased stocks.

11. Which of the following was NOT a cause of the Great Depression?
    - (A) The stock market crashed.
    - (B) High tariffs were placed on imported and exported goods.
    - (C) Many people borrowed money from banks, which they could not pay back.
    - (D) There was a sharp increase in the price of manufactured goods.

12. Which of the following describes a way in which the Great Depression affected the lives of many Americans?
    - (A) Many people moved from shantytowns to suburbs.
    - (B) Many children quit school to help their families earn money.
    - (C) More people got married immediately after high school or college.
    - (D) Farmers were hurt by the effects of tariffs and rising crop prices.

13. Which New Deal program provided monthly payments to the elderly, disabled, and unemployed?
    - (A) Farm Security Administration
    - (B) Social Security
    - (C) Securities and Exchange Commission
    - (D) Works Progress Administration

14. What was an effect of the Dust Bowl?
    - (A) Many factories laid off workers.
    - (B) Many families left California and headed east.
    - (C) Many people became migrant workers.
    - (D) Many farmers moved to the Great Plains.

15. Which new form of entertainment in the
1930s included characters such as
Superman and Batman?
Ⓐ the movie
Ⓑ the World's Fair
Ⓒ the board game
Ⓓ the comic book

Part 2: Skills Test

Directions: Use complete sentences to answer questions 1–5. Use a separate sheet
of paper if you need more space.

1. Complete the chart below. Use the details to draw a conclusion about the effects of mass
media in the United States. **Draw Conclusions**

Detail: People throughout the country bought the same products that were advertised on the radio.	Detail: The same songs, shows, and movies became popular across the entire nation.	Detail: Many people copied the hairstyles and clothing of their favorite movie stars.

Conclusion:

2. What were some effects of the Eighteenth Amendment? **Cause and Effect**

_____

_____

_____

_____

_____

3. Read the passage. Write one fact and one opinion in the space provided. **Fact and Opinion**

> **F. Scott Fitzgerald was a talented writer. His novels include *This Side of Paradise*, *The Great Gatsby*, and *Tender Is the Night*. *The Great Gatsby* is by far his best work. It tells a story about New York life during the Roaring Twenties.**

Fact:

Opinion:

4. How did Franklin D. Roosevelt try to help the country through the Great Depression? **Summarize**

_____

_____

_____

_____

_____

_____

5. What caused the Dust Bowl? **Cause and Effect**

_____

_____

_____

_____

Chapter 8 Test

Part 1: Content Test

Directions: Fill in the circle next to the correct answer.

1. Why did Great Britain and France declare war on Germany?
   - Ⓐ Germany invaded Poland.
   - Ⓑ Germany invaded Austria and Czechoslovakia.
   - Ⓒ Germany formed an alliance with Italy and Japan.
   - Ⓓ Adolf Hitler became the dictator of Germany.

2. Why did the rise of dictators cause concern in the 1930s?
   - Ⓐ Countries ruled by dictators became vulnerable to attack.
   - Ⓑ Dictators placed high tariffs on imported goods.
   - Ⓒ Dictators believed in a weak central government.
   - Ⓓ Dictators often planned to attack and conquer other countries.

3. What event caused the United States to enter World War II?
   - Ⓐ Germany bombed Great Britain.
   - Ⓑ Japan bombed Pearl Harbor.
   - Ⓒ Germany took over much of Western Europe.
   - Ⓓ Japan took over much of China and Southeast Asia.

4. Who were the Axis powers during World War II?
   - Ⓐ the United States, Great Britain, and France
   - Ⓑ the United States, Great Britain, France, and the Soviet Union
   - Ⓒ Germany, Italy, and Japan
   - Ⓓ Germany, Italy, Japan, and the Soviet Union

5. Which of the following describes an effect of World War II on the United States economy?
   - Ⓐ Automobile companies produced a record number of cars.
   - Ⓑ Many factories had to expand to produce military equipment.
   - Ⓒ The airplane industry suffered as the Allies began using airplanes in combat.
   - Ⓓ Cities with shipyards declined because so many ships had been sent overseas.

6. Which of the following does NOT describe a role of women during World War II?
   - Ⓐ pilots
   - Ⓑ factory workers
   - Ⓒ soldiers
   - Ⓓ mechanics

7. Where did the first African American fighter pilots begin training?
   Ⓐ Norfolk, Virginia
   Ⓑ Los Alamos, New Mexico
   Ⓒ Manhattan, New York
   Ⓓ Tuskegee, Alabama

8. Which of the following best describes Executive Order #9066?
   Ⓐ It forced many Japanese Americans to move to internment camps.
   Ⓑ It forced many Japanese Americans to leave the United States.
   Ⓒ It allowed many Japanese Americans to join the United States military.
   Ⓓ It allowed many Japanese Americans to become citizens.

9. What was the Manhattan Project?
   Ⓐ the world's first computer
   Ⓑ a complicated code machine used by the German military
   Ⓒ the effort by the United States to build an atomic bomb
   Ⓓ radio beams used to determine the locations of objects

10. After which battle did Japan's navy become too weak to continue capturing islands in the Pacific?
    Ⓐ Battle of Midway
    Ⓑ Battle of Stalingrad
    Ⓒ Battle of the Bulge
    Ⓓ Battle of Iwo Jima

11. After which battle was Germany forced to retreat from the Soviet Union?
    Ⓐ Battle of Midway
    Ⓑ Battle of Stalingrad
    Ⓒ Battle of the Bulge
    Ⓓ Battle of Iwo Jima

12. Where did the largest sea invasion in world history take place?
    Ⓐ Hiroshima, Japan
    Ⓑ Nagasaki, Japan
    Ⓒ Berlin, Germany
    Ⓓ Normandy, France

13. How did the use of atomic bombs impact the outcome of World War II?
    Ⓐ Germany was forced to surrender.
    Ⓑ Germany was forced to retreat from Western Europe.
    Ⓒ Japan was forced to surrender.
    Ⓓ Japan was forced to retreat from the Pacific Islands.

14. What were concentration camps?
    Ⓐ places where Jews and others were imprisoned and murdered
    Ⓑ ghettos in which many Jews were forced to live
    Ⓒ places where Japanese Americans were relocated
    Ⓓ secret hiding places where people hid from the Nazis

15. About how many Jews were murdered during the Holocaust?
    Ⓐ six hundred
    Ⓑ six thousand
    Ⓒ six hundred thousand
    Ⓓ six million

Part 2: Skills Test

Directions: Use complete sentences to answer questions 1–5. Use a separate sheet
of paper if you need more space.

1. How did World War II change life for many women and African Americans? **Summarize**

_____

_____

_____

_____

_____

_____

2. Complete the chart below. Use the details to draw a conclusion about Americans on the
home front during World War II. **Draw Conclusions**

Detail: Many children organized "scrap drives."	Detail: Millions of Americans planted Victory Gardens.	Detail: Families rationed goods.

Conclusion:

3. Why did President Truman decide to use the atomic bomb? **Main Idea and Details**

_____

_____

_____

4. Write the following events in the order in which they happened. **Sequence**

Allied forces led an invasion in Normandy, France.

George S. Patton led the Allies to victory at the Battle of the Bulge.

The Allies defeated Axis forces in North Africa and Italy.

_____

_____

_____

_____

5. Look at the map below. Describe the location of the equator. Which two World War II battles took place closest to the equator? **Understand Key Lines of Latitude and Longitude**

_____

_____

_____

_____

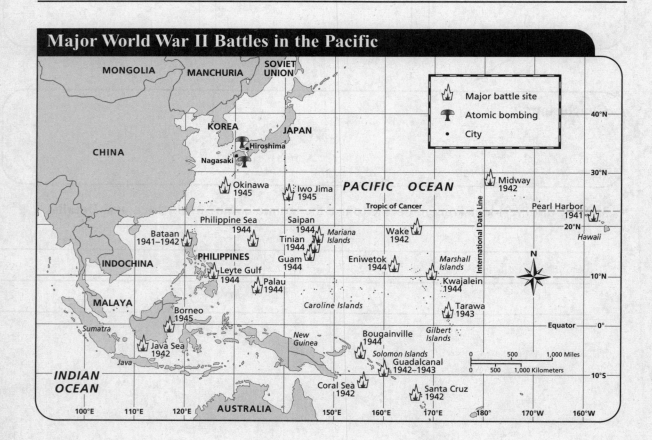

Major World War II Battles in the Pacific

Unit 4 Test

Part 1: Content Test

Directions: Fill in the circle next to the correct answer.

1. How did the assembly line change American industry?
   - (A) It increased the cost of manufactured products.
   - (B) It allowed companies to manufacture large numbers of identical products.
   - (C) It caused an increase in unemployment.
   - (D) It forced many factory workers to take a cut in pay.

2. How did the automobile change life in the United States?
   - (A) Many farmers were unable to get their crops to market.
   - (B) Many people were able to move closer to their jobs.
   - (C) The manufacture of automobiles helped create many new jobs.
   - (D) The increase in car ownership led to a decline in tourism.

3. Which event did NOT lead to the passage of the Eighteenth Amendment?
   - (A) Many were concerned that people abused alcohol.
   - (B) Many were concerned that people spent money on alcohol instead of on their families.
   - (C) Progressive reformers helped pass Blue Laws.
   - (D) Bootleggers competed for business with the speakeasies.

4. Which of the following describes the achievements of Zora Neale Hurston?
   - (A) created several series of paintings that showed African American life and history
   - (B) wrote about the experiences of African Americans
   - (C) made several recordings with Louis Armstrong
   - (D) wrote concert music such as "Rhapsody in Blue"

5. During the stock market crash of 1929
   - (A) many investors panicked and purchased stocks.
   - (B) many investors panicked and sold their stocks.
   - (C) the market froze because people were afraid to buy or sell stocks.
   - (D) stock prices rose and investors could no longer afford them.

6. Which of the following was a cause of the Great Depression?
   - (A) Many investors had purchased stocks on credit.
   - (B) Congress reduced tariffs on foreign goods.
   - (C) Many farmers were unable to produce enough crops.
   - (D) Many factories faced a shortage of workers.

7. Which New Deal program was set up to protect investors in the stock market?
   Ⓐ Social Security
   Ⓑ Securities and Exchange Commission
   Ⓒ Works Progress Administration
   Ⓓ Civilian Conservation Corps

8. What caused the Dust Bowl?
   Ⓐ long periods of heavy rain
   Ⓑ lack of sunshine
   Ⓒ severe thunderstorms
   Ⓓ severe drought and high winds

9. What was an effect of Japan's attack on Pearl Harbor?
   Ⓐ The United States declared war on Japan.
   Ⓑ The United States allowed Britain to borrow military supplies.
   Ⓒ Japan gained control of China and Southeast Asia.
   Ⓓ Japan joined an alliance with Germany and Italy.

10. Who were the major Allied Powers during World War II?
    Ⓐ Germany, Italy, and Japan
    Ⓑ Germany, Italy, Japan, and the Soviet Union
    Ⓒ the United States, Britain, France, and Poland
    Ⓓ the United States, Britain, France, and the Soviet Union

11. Which of the following does NOT describe an effect of World War II on the United States?
    Ⓐ Many automobile companies went out of business.
    Ⓑ Many cities with busy shipyards became boom towns.
    Ⓒ The country faced food shortages.
    Ⓓ Many women and African Americans were faced with new opportunities.

12. Enigma was
    Ⓐ the effort by the United States to build an atomic bomb.
    Ⓑ a complicated code machine used by the German military.
    Ⓒ the world's first computer.
    Ⓓ a radio beam used to determine the location of ships.

13. At which battle did General George S. Patton lead the Allies to victory against Germany?
    Ⓐ Battle of Midway
    Ⓑ Battle of Stalingrad
    Ⓒ Battle of the Bulge
    Ⓓ Battle of Iwo Jima

14. The use of the atomic bomb
    Ⓐ saved many Japanese lives.
    Ⓑ prevented Japan from invading the United States.
    Ⓒ helped force Japan to surrender.
    Ⓓ made an invasion of Japan necessary.

15. During the Holocaust
　Ⓐ about one million Jews were
　　murdered.
　Ⓑ about two million Jews were
　　murdered.
　Ⓒ about four million Jews were
　　murdered.
　Ⓓ about six million Jews were
　　murdered.

Part 2: Skills Test

Directions: Use complete sentences to answer questions 1–5. Use a separate sheet
of paper if you need more space.

1. Read the passage. Write one fact and one opinion in the space provided. **Fact and Opinion**

> **On November 2, 1920, the first professional radio station in the world began
> broadcasting. This was an exciting day. Listeners were able to hear results of the U.S.
> presidential election. Radio stations soon began broadcasting music, dramas, and
> even sports programs. The best radio program was the action-adventure**
> ***Captain Midnight.***

Fact:

Opinion:

2. What is the purpose of using lines of latitude and longitude? What is the latitude of the
equator? **Understand Key Lines of Latitude and Longitude**

_____

_____

3. Complete the chart below. Use the details to draw a conclusion about why Prohibition ended. **Draw Conclusions**

| **Detail: Some bootleggers sold alcohol that was dangerous.** | **Detail: Competition between bootleggers often led to violent clashes.** | **Detail: Police had little success in stopping bootleggers.** |

Conclusion:

4. How did the Great Depression affect the lives of many Americans? **Summarize**

_____

_____

5. Write the following events in the order in which they happened. **Sequence**

Germany invaded Poland.

Britain and France declared war on Germany.

Germany formed an alliance with Italy and Japan.

Chapter 9 Test

Part 1: Content Test

Directions: Fill in the circle next to the correct answer.

1. Which of the following does NOT describe Europe after World War II?
   - Ⓐ Germany emerged as one of the world's most powerful nations.
   - Ⓑ Industries, farms, and homes were in ruins.
   - Ⓒ Many people were without food, clothing, and shelter.
   - Ⓓ Much of Eastern Europe fell to Soviet control.

2. What was a main goal of the Marshall Plan?
   - Ⓐ to encourage the spread of communism in Europe
   - Ⓑ to help Europe recover from the war
   - Ⓒ to help Japan recover from the war
   - Ⓓ to help Japan set up a democratic government

3. Which of the following describes the United States after World War II?
   - Ⓐ Much of the United States was in ruins.
   - Ⓑ The United States emerged from the war as one of the world's weakest nations.
   - Ⓒ The United States gained control of Japan and Eastern Europe.
   - Ⓓ The United States emerged from the war as a superpower.

4. What was a main purpose in forming the United Nations?
   - Ⓐ to create a plan for rebuilding Europe and Japan
   - Ⓑ to create an organization that would promote global cooperation
   - Ⓒ to create an iron curtain between communist and noncommunist countries
   - Ⓓ to create a military alliance against the Soviet Union

5. What was the Cold War?
   - Ⓐ a long, bitter struggle between the United States and the Soviet Union
   - Ⓑ an armed conflict between the United States and the Soviet Union
   - Ⓒ a period in which many Asian and European nations established communist governments
   - Ⓓ a period in which many Free World nations became Third World nations

6. Which of the following describes a difference in ideology between Soviets and Americans?
   - Ⓐ Soviets believed in free enterprise and Americans believed in democracy.
   - Ⓑ Soviets believed in communism and Americans believed in little personal freedom.
   - Ⓒ Soviets believed in communism and Americans believed in democracy.
   - Ⓓ Soviets wanted to work for peace and Americans wanted an iron curtain.

7. Which of the following did NOT contribute to the growth of the American economy following World War II?
   (A) Many families wanted to buy new homes.
   (B) The number of returning veterans resulted in a shortage of jobs.
   (C) Industries could focus on producing consumer goods instead of war materials.
   (D) Rationing had ended.

8. Which of the following is NOT a way in which Americans changed the way they lived in the 1950s?
   (A) Many placed a greater emphasis on education.
   (B) Many used credit cards to charge goods and services.
   (C) Many moved from suburbs to cities.
   (D) Many enjoyed more leisure time.

9. Which statement describes the automotive industry in the 1950s?
   (A) The automotive industry declined because public transportation became more widely available.
   (B) The automotive industry declined as focus shifted from developing peacetime technologies to war technologies.
   (C) Many engineers left the automotive industry to design fighter planes.
   (D) New technologies such as automatic transmission, radial tires, and power steering were introduced.

10. Which of the following is NOT a way in which new technologies changed life for Americans in the 1950s?
    (A) Most households had Internet access.
    (B) Most households had televisions.
    (C) Many households had air conditioning systems.
    (D) Many people began to use commercial airlines.

11. Which event led to the Korean War?
    (A) South Koreans invaded communist North Korea.
    (B) Communist North Koreans invaded South Korea.
    (C) The United States and its allies invaded communist South Korea.
    (D) Communist Chinese forces invaded South Korea.

12. Which of the following occurred at the end of the Korean War?
    (A) Korea was united under a democratic government.
    (B) Korea was united under a communist government.
    (C) United States troops helped guard the border zone between North Korea and South Korea.
    (D) Chinese troops helped guard the border zone between North Korea and South Korea.

13. What was the purpose of the Southeast Asia Treaty Organization?

Ⓐ to ease Cold War tensions between the United States and the Soviet Union

Ⓑ to form an alliance against the United States

Ⓒ to create a blockade against western nations

Ⓓ to protect Southeast Asian countries against the spread of communism

14. Which of the following did NOT occur during the Red Scare?

Ⓐ Many communists were arrested.

Ⓑ Many innocent people were investigated and sometimes bullied.

Ⓒ Investigators learned that Senator Joseph McCarthy was a communist spy.

Ⓓ People who refused to cooperate with investigations often lost their jobs.

15. Which event led to the Cuban Missile Crisis?

Ⓐ Soviets were setting up nuclear missiles in Cuba.

Ⓑ Cubans were setting up nuclear missiles in the Soviet Union.

Ⓒ The United States formed an alliance with Cuba against the Soviet Union.

Ⓓ The Soviet Union and the United States agreed to stop building nuclear weapons.

Part 2: Skills Test

Directions: Use complete sentences to answer questions 1–5. Use a separate sheet of paper if you need more space.

1. In what ways were the United States and the Soviet Union similar after World War II? In what ways were they different? **Compare and Contrast**

_____

_____

_____

_____

_____

2. Complete the cause and effect chart below. Identify a cause of the Berlin Airlift.
Cause and Effect

> **Cause:**

↓

> **Effect: The Americans and British flew food and fuel into West Berlin.**

3. Describe the similarities and differences between primary and secondary sources.
Compare Primary and Secondary Sources

_____

_____

_____

_____

_____

4. How did the G.I. Bill of Rights help men and women who had served in the military?
Main Idea and Details

_____

_____

_____

_____

5. Why do you think American leaders felt it was important to stay ahead of the Soviet Union in the arms race? **Draw Conclusions**

_____

_____

_____

_____

Chapter 10 Test

Part 1: Content Test

Directions: Fill in the circle next to the correct answer.

1. Which of the following was a cause of the civil rights movement?
   - (A) African Americans were often denied equal rights.
   - (B) President Roosevelt ordered an end to discrimination in all defense industries.
   - (C) Many were upset with the Supreme Court's decision in *Brown* v. *Board of Education*.
   - (D) Congress passed the Voting Rights Act of 1964.

2. Which of the following is NOT a way in which segregation affected American society?
   - (A) Blacks and whites had to attend separate schools.
   - (B) Blacks and whites were socially isolated.
   - (C) Blacks and whites had to use separate public facilities.
   - (D) Blacks and whites had to ride different public buses.

3. Which of the following events occurred last?
   - (A) President Truman ordered an end to segregation of the United States military.
   - (B) Martin Luther King, Jr., helped plan a massive march in Washington, D.C.
   - (C) Rosa Parks refused to give up her seat on a Montgomery bus.
   - (D) Segregation of public schools was declared illegal.

4. Which of the following describes the Civil Rights Act of 1964?
   - (A) Supreme Court ruling that segregation of public buses was illegal
   - (B) Supreme Court ruling that protected the rights of all Americans to vote
   - (C) law passed by Congress that banned segregation in all public places in the United States
   - (D) law passed by Congress that banned the use of passive resistance

5. What was the space race?
   - (A) race between the United States and the Soviet Union to build weapons
   - (B) race between the United States and China to gain control of Asian territory
   - (C) race between the United States and the Soviet Union to explore outer space
   - (D) race between the United States and China to explore outer space

6. Why did the United States send soldiers to Vietnam?
   - (A) North Vietnamese were fighting to unite Vietnam under a communist government.
   - (B) South Vietnamese were fighting to unite Vietnam under a communist government.
   - (C) The Soviet Union had sent forces into South Vietnam.
   - (D) China had gained control of North Vietnam and threatened to invade South Vietnam.

7. Which of the following did NOT occur after the last American troops left Vietnam?
   Ⓐ The North Vietnamese and the South Vietnamese continued fighting.
   Ⓑ South Vietnam surrendered to North Vietnam.
   Ⓒ Henry Kissinger met with North Vietnamese and Viet Cong leaders in Paris.
   Ⓓ Vietnam was united under a communist government.

8. Which statement best describes the doves' position toward the Vietnam Conflict?
   Ⓐ They believed it was a civil war that should be settled by the Vietnamese people.
   Ⓑ They believed it was a civil war that should be settled by China and the Soviet Union.
   Ⓒ They believed it was necessary to stop the spread of communism.
   Ⓓ They believed the United States should station troops along the Chinese border.

9. Which statement best describes the role of women in the mid-1900s?
   Ⓐ Women had the same opportunities as men.
   Ⓑ The number of women in the workplace continued to decrease.
   Ⓒ Women often earned higher wages than men.
   Ⓓ Women were not allowed to participate in certain sports.

10. Which of the following is NOT an achievement of the Women's Rights Movement of the mid-1900s?
    Ⓐ The National Organization for Women was formed.
    Ⓑ Congress passed the Title 9 law.
    Ⓒ The Equal Rights Amendment was ratified.
    Ⓓ More job opportunities became available for women.

11. What was the purpose of the National Farm Workers Association?
    Ⓐ to gain rights for Americans with disabilities
    Ⓑ to gain rights for migrant workers
    Ⓒ to gain rights for American Indians
    Ⓓ to gain rights for Japanese Americans

12. Which of the following is NOT a way in which Americans worked to improve the environment in the late 1900s?
    Ⓐ The Environmental Protection Agency was formed.
    Ⓑ Congress passed mandatory recycling laws.
    Ⓒ The first Earth Day was celebrated.
    Ⓓ Rachel Carson wrote *Silent Spring*.

13. Which statement does NOT describe President Nixon's trip to China?
    Ⓐ It was the first time an American President visited China.
    Ⓑ It was an important step toward friendlier relations with China.
    Ⓒ Nixon signed an arms control agreement with Chinese leaders.
    Ⓓ Nixon met with communist leader Mao Zedong.

14. Why did President Carter invite the leaders of Egypt and Israel to the United States?

Ⓐ to form a military alliance with the two nations

Ⓑ to try to improve trade relations with the two nations

Ⓒ to help the two nations overthrow their communist governments

Ⓓ to try to help bring peace between the two nations

15. Which of the following did NOT lead to the collapse of communism in the 1990s?

Ⓐ Cold War tensions increased.

Ⓑ The Soviet economy was weakened by the high cost of the arms race.

Ⓒ Mikhail Gorbachev came to power.

Ⓓ People in Eastern Europe gained more freedom.

Part 2: Skills Test

Directions: Use complete sentences to answer questions 1–5. Use a separate sheet of paper if you need more space.

1. Identify three ways in which African Americans used passive resistance to gain civil rights. **Main Idea and Details**

_____

2. Explain how the Vietnam Conflict divided many Americans. **Summarize**

_____

_____

_____

_____

3. Write the following events in the order in which they happened. **Sequence**

The Berlin Wall was destroyed.

The United States and the Soviet Union agreed to destroy some of their nuclear weapons.

The Soviet Union broke up into 15 independent republics.

Communist governments fell in several Eastern European nations.

_____

_____

_____

_____

4. Complete the cause-and-effect chart below. Identify an effect of Iraq's invasion of Kuwait. **Cause and Effect**

> **Cause:** Saddam Hussein refused to withdraw his troops from Kuwait.

> **Effect:**

5. Study the maps below. Describe the differences between the two maps. **Understand Map Projections**

_____

_____

_____

_____

_____

_____

Equal-Area Projection

Mercator Projection

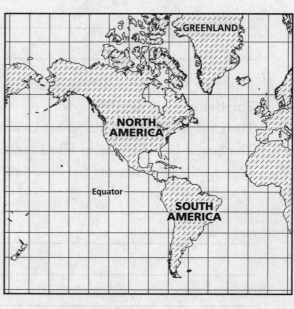

Unit 5 Test

Part 1: Content Test

Directions: Fill in the circle next to the correct answer.

1. Which of the following describes Japan after World War II?
   - Ⓐ Japan adopted a communist government.
   - Ⓑ Japan adopted a democratic government.
   - Ⓒ Japan was divided into North Japan and South Japan.
   - Ⓓ Japan emerged from the war as one of the world's most powerful nations.

2. Which statement describes the role of the United States after World War II?
   - Ⓐ Victory, military strength, and resources made the United States a superpower.
   - Ⓑ The United States demanded control over its bordering countries.
   - Ⓒ The United States controlled much of Eastern and Central Europe.
   - Ⓓ The United States stationed advisors in the Soviet Union to help with their recovery.

3. Which of the following describes a cause of Cold War tensions?
   - Ⓐ The Soviet Union believed in personal freedoms and the United States did not.
   - Ⓑ The Soviet Union believed in free enterprise and the United States did not.
   - Ⓒ The United States supported communism and the Soviet Union did not.
   - Ⓓ The United States supported freely elected governments and the Soviet Union did not.

4. Which of the following contributed to the rapid growth of the American economy after World War II?
   - Ⓐ Many felt confident about the future and began spending more money.
   - Ⓑ Industries that had produced consumer goods were able to focus on producing war materials.
   - Ⓒ Many people moved from suburbs to cities.
   - Ⓓ Many families rationed goods such as food and clothing.

5. Which of the following is NOT a new technology that improved life for Americans in the 1950s?
   - Ⓐ air conditioning
   - Ⓑ better heating systems
   - Ⓒ coast-to-coast direct dial telephone service
   - Ⓓ electric streetcar

6. How did the Korean War relate to the Cold War?
   - Ⓐ The Soviet Union joined South Korean forces to help stop the spread of democracy.
   - Ⓑ The Soviet union joined North Korean forces to help stop the spread of communism.
   - Ⓒ The United States joined South Korean forces to help stop the spread of communism.
   - Ⓓ The United States joined North Korean forces to help stop the spread of democracy.

7. How did Cold War tensions affect Americans at home?
   Ⓐ All Americans were forced to take an oath of loyalty to the government.
   Ⓑ Americans were not allowed to travel outside of United States borders.
   Ⓒ Communist revolutions took place in several major cities.
   Ⓓ Many feared that communist spies were working inside the government.

8. How did President Kennedy respond to information that the Soviets were setting up nuclear missiles in Cuba?
   Ⓐ He insisted that the Soviets remove their missiles.
   Ⓑ He signed a peace treaty with Fidel Castro.
   Ⓒ He declared that the United States would set up missiles along Soviet borders.
   Ⓓ He ordered an attack on the Soviet Union.

9. Which of the following was a direct effect of Rosa Parks's refusal to give up her seat on a Montgomery bus?
   Ⓐ Freedom rides were organized to see if public transportation was obeying the law.
   Ⓑ Sit-ins were held at lunch counters and other public places across the South.
   Ⓒ Martin Luther King, Jr., helped organize a massive march in Washington, D.C.
   Ⓓ Civil rights leaders organized a boycott on Montgomery buses.

10. The Civil Rights Act of 1964
    Ⓐ banned segregation in all public places.
    Ⓑ protected the rights of voters.
    Ⓒ made sit-ins and freedom rides illegal.
    Ⓓ outlawed segregation of the United States military.

11. Who became the first American to orbit Earth?
    Ⓐ Yuri Gagarin
    Ⓑ John Glenn
    Ⓒ Neil Armstrong
    Ⓓ Michael Collins

12. What caused the United States to send troops to fight in Vietnam?
    Ⓐ Vietnamese soldiers who had fought for the French began moving north.
    Ⓑ Soviet and Chinese forces were trying to gain control of North Vietnam.
    Ⓒ Ho Chi Minh's forces were winning the war against South Vietnam.
    Ⓓ The South Vietnamese were winning the war against the Viet Cong.

13. Which of the following describes the National Organization for Women?
    Ⓐ an amendment that stated everyone must be treated exactly the same
    Ⓑ an organization that worked toward equal opportunities for women
    Ⓒ an organization that used passive resistance to gain rights for migrant workers
    Ⓓ a law stating that federally funded public schools must offer equal opportunities to men and women

14. Which of the following describes the Civil Liberties Act of 1988?

Ⓐ ensures that no one is denied employment on the basis of race or sex

Ⓑ makes it illegal to refuse to hire a qualified person because that person has a disability

Ⓒ apologized for the injustice endured by Japanese Americans during World War II

Ⓓ rewarded Native Americans who served as code talkers during World War II

15. Which of the following contributed to the collapse of communism in Europe?

Ⓐ The high cost of the arms race weakened the Soviet economy.

Ⓑ Mikhail Gorbachev allowed less political and economic freedom than previous leaders.

Ⓒ Cold War tensions increased between the United States and the Soviet Union.

Ⓓ The Soviet Union refused to agree to an arms control agreement.

Part 2: Skills Test

Directions: Use complete sentences to answer questions 1–5. Use a separate sheet of paper if you need more space.

1. What was the main goal in forming the United Nations? **Summarize**

_____

_____

_____

2. Complete the cause-and-effect chart below. Write an effect of the Voting Rights Act of 1965. **Cause and Effect**

Cause: The Voting Rights Act of 1965 protected the rights of all Americans to vote.

Effect:

3. Identify two factors that made the Vietnam Conflict one of the most difficult wars ever fought by Americans. **Main Idea and Details**

_____

_____

_____

4. Suppose you wanted to find out what it was like to be a soldier in the Korean War. Do you think a primary or secondary source would be more helpful? Explain. **Compare Primary and Secondary Sources**

_____

_____

_____

5. Study the maps below. Which map would you use to compare the actual sizes of Greenland and South America? Explain. **Understand Map Projections**

_____

_____

_____

Equal-Area Projection

Mercator Projection

Chapter 11 Test

Part 1: Content Test

Directions: Fill in the circle next to the correct answer.

1. Which region of the United States includes Kansas and Nebraska?
   - Ⓐ West
   - Ⓑ Midwest
   - Ⓒ Southwest
   - Ⓓ Southeast

2. Which of the following describes a reason why the population of the Sunbelt increased rapidly?
   - Ⓐ Other regions were overcrowded and did not accept immigrants.
   - Ⓑ Many businesses moved there to take advantage of its natural resources.
   - Ⓒ Many workers moved there to take advantage of lower wages.
   - Ⓓ The invention of modern heating systems made it a more comfortable place to live.

3. *E Pluribus Unum* means
   - Ⓐ "Out of many, one."
   - Ⓑ "I came, I saw, I conquered."
   - Ⓒ "For the people, by the people."
   - Ⓓ "Seize the day."

4. Since the late 1900s, most immigrants have come from
   - Ⓐ Europe or Africa.
   - Ⓑ Europe or Asia.
   - Ⓒ Latin America or Asia.
   - Ⓓ Latin America or Africa.

5. Which statement describes how the republican system of government works in the United States?
   - Ⓐ Each individual has the opportunity to vote on every decision the government makes.
   - Ⓑ The judicial branch makes the laws and the legislative branch runs the government.
   - Ⓒ Citizens elect representatives to make laws and run the government.
   - Ⓓ Citizens elect a President to make laws and run the government.

6. Which of the following is NOT a responsibility of citizenship?
   - Ⓐ enforcing laws
   - Ⓑ paying taxes
   - Ⓒ serving on a jury
   - Ⓓ voting

7. A 17-year-old citizen has all of the following basic rights EXCEPT
   - Ⓐ freedom of religion.
   - Ⓑ freedom of speech.
   - Ⓒ the right to vote.
   - Ⓓ the right to a fair trial.

8. Which statement is true about the process for electing the President of the United States?
   - Ⓐ The number of electoral votes a candidate receives is based on the number of senators in each state.
   - Ⓑ Electors are appointed by the Supreme Court to determine who will become President.
   - Ⓒ It is possible for a candidate to win the electoral vote but still lose the election.
   - Ⓓ It is possible for a candidate to win a majority of the popular vote but still lose the election.

9. Why is the Constitution called a living document?
   - Ⓐ Its authors are still living.
   - Ⓑ It can be changed over time.
   - Ⓒ It states that Supreme Court justices are appointed for life.
   - Ⓓ Only Supreme Court justices are allowed to add amendments.

10. How does supply and demand affect businesses?
   - Ⓐ Consumers will only buy a product if the supply is high.
   - Ⓑ Supply and demand increases the opportunity cost of making a product.
   - Ⓒ Businesses can charge more if supply is high and demand is limited.
   - Ⓓ Businesses can charge more if supply is limited and demand is high.

11. Which of the following had the greatest effect on the business and job markets in the late 1900s?
   - Ⓐ the computer
   - Ⓑ the invention of automobiles
   - Ⓒ the introduction of electricity
   - Ⓓ the aging population

12. About what percentage of students between the ages of five and seventeen used computers in 2001?
   - Ⓐ 30 percent
   - Ⓑ 50 percent
   - Ⓒ 75 percent
   - Ⓓ 90 percent

13. Which statement describes how the trading policies of the United States have changed in the late twentieth century?
   - Ⓐ The United States banned international trade.
   - Ⓑ The United States signed trade agreements with several countries.
   - Ⓒ The United States discouraged trade by placing higher tariffs on imports and exports.
   - Ⓓ The United States stopped trading with all countries except Canada and Mexico.

14. Which of the following describes a result of globalization?
    Ⓐ What happens to the economy in one country can affect the economy in other countries.
    Ⓑ The system of free enterprise fails because competition no longer exists.
    Ⓒ People and goods move less freely from one country to another.
    Ⓓ The cultures of other countries become more isolated.

15. Which of the following describes an effect of the interdependence between China and the United States after the Cold War?
    Ⓐ The price of manufactured goods in the United States increased.
    Ⓑ Many workers in China lost their jobs.
    Ⓒ Companies and consumers in both countries suffered losses.
    Ⓓ Companies and consumers in both countries profited.

Part 2: Skills Test

Directions: Use complete sentences to answer questions 1–5. Use a separate sheet of paper if you need more space.

1. Describe some effects of the growing diversity of immigrants that have come to the United States since the late 1900s. **Cause and Effect**

    _____

    _____

    _____

2. Complete the chart below. Summarize the details about the different ways to be an active citizen. **Summarize**

Detail: You can volunteer to help political candidates.	**Detail: You can take part in a community project.**	**Detail: You can write or call political leaders to express your opinions.**

    Summary:

3. What is the North American Free Trade Agreement? **Summarize**

_____

_____

_____

4. Suppose you want to find out more about the effects of globalization. Describe how you would use the Internet to research your topic. **Internet Research**

_____

_____

_____

5. How would you use population density maps to compare two different regions of the United States? **Compare Population Density Maps**

_____

_____

_____

_____

_____

Chapter 12 Test

Part 1: Content Test

Directions: Fill in the circle next to the correct answer.

1. Which of the following events occurred on September 11, 2001?
   - Ⓐ Terrorists crashed two planes into the twin towers of the World Trade Center.
   - Ⓑ Terrorists crashed two planes into the Pentagon.
   - Ⓒ Terrorists crashed a plane into the Capitol building.
   - Ⓓ Terrorists crashed a plane into the White House.

2. About how many people were killed by the terrorist acts on September 11, 2001?
   - Ⓐ 1,500
   - Ⓑ 3,000
   - Ⓒ 5,000
   - Ⓓ 6,000

3. Why are firefighters, police officers, and rescue workers remembered as heroes for their actions on September 11, 2001?
   - Ⓐ They collected toys and sent them to children who had lost loved ones.
   - Ⓑ They lined up to give blood to help those injured in the attacks.
   - Ⓒ They guided thousands of people to safety.
   - Ⓓ They delivered food and money to families in need.

4. Why did the United States take military action against Afghanistan?
   - Ⓐ The Taliban organized the attacks of September 11, 2001.
   - Ⓑ The Taliban refused to capture Osama bin Laden and other al Qaeda leaders.
   - Ⓒ The Taliban carried out several attacks against American targets.
   - Ⓓ The Taliban opposed American influence in Western and Central Asia.

5. Which event occurred in Afghanistan?
   - Ⓐ The United States captured Osama bin Laden and other al Qaeda leaders.
   - Ⓑ The Taliban captured Osama bin Laden and other al Qaeda leaders.
   - Ⓒ The United States worked with the Taliban to remove al Qaeda from power.
   - Ⓓ The Taliban was forced to surrender power.

6. What happened when Saddam Hussein was again forced to admit weapons inspectors into Iraq?
   - Ⓐ Inspectors could not determine whether Iraq had weapons of mass destruction.
   - Ⓑ Inspectors found weapons that spread deadly diseases.
   - Ⓒ Inspectors found weapons that spread poison chemicals.
   - Ⓓ Inspectors found nuclear weapons.

7. Why did American forces bomb Baghdad on March 20, 2003?
   - (A) Iraq invaded Kuwait.
   - (B) Iraq attacked the United States.
   - (C) The United States wanted to remove Saddam Hussein from power.
   - (D) Osama bin Laden was hiding in Baghdad.

8. Which of the following might help protect the environment?
   - (A) relying on nuclear power
   - (B) burning more gasoline and coal
   - (C) increasing the amount of carbon dioxide that is released in the atmosphere
   - (D) decreasing the amount of carbon dioxide that is released in the atmosphere

9. How might a car that runs on hydrogen fuel help protect the environment?
   - (A) by releasing gases that would cool the global climate
   - (B) by not producing air pollution
   - (C) by eliminating the need for roads and highways
   - (D) by releasing gases that would improve the atmosphere

10. In 2000, about how many people in the world lived on less than $1 a day?
   - (A) five thousand
   - (B) one million
   - (C) five million
   - (D) one billion

11. Where do most cases of malaria occur?
   - (A) Africa
   - (B) Australia
   - (C) Europe
   - (D) the United States

12. What is Acquired Immunodeficiency Syndrome?
   - (A) a disease that is caused by hunger
   - (B) a disease that is caused by poverty
   - (C) a disease that attacks people's immune systems
   - (D) a disease that is spread by mosquitoes

13. In what ways has Jimmy Carter worked to solve global problems?
   - (A) by supporting free elections and helping to fight disease
   - (B) by accepting the Nobel Peace Prize
   - (C) by making a list of "Development Goals"
   - (D) by developing medicines to fight malaria and AIDS

14. What do scientists at the University of Southern California hope to use to help people with brain damage?
   - (A) artificial intelligence
   - (B) computer chips
   - (C) jet airplanes
   - (D) Martian rocks and soil

15. What do scientists at NASA hope to develop by the year 2014?
   - (A) satellites that can take pictures of Earth
   - (B) a spacecraft that can orbit Earth
   - (C) a spacecraft that can travel to Mars and bring samples back to Earth
   - (D) a spacecraft that can travel to the moon

Part 2: Skills Test

Directions: Use complete sentences to answer questions 1–5. Use a separate sheet of paper if you need more space.

1. Read the passage. Write a sentence that is a generalization of the information in the passage. **Make Generalizations**

> After the attacks of September 11, 2001, people all over the country lined up to give blood to help injured victims. Millions of people donated food, clothing, and money. Firefighters and other workers from cities and towns across the United States drove to New York City to help with the rescue effort.

_____

_____

2. What is al Qaeda and how has it affected the United States? **Main Idea and Details**

_____

_____

_____

_____

3. Why did some people support the use of military force against Iraq? Why did others believe that war was not necessary? **Compare and Contrast**

_____

_____

_____

_____

_____

_____

4. What is global warming? Why are some scientists concerned about its effects? **Summarize**

_____

_____

_____

_____

5. Complete the chart below. Summarize the details about the global challenges people are working to solve. **Summarize**

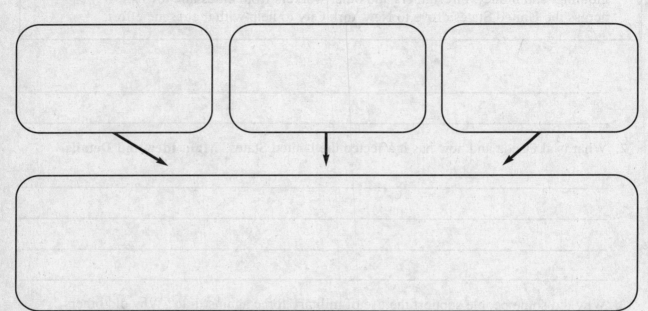

Unit 6 Test

Part 1: Content Test

Directions: Fill in the circle next to the correct answer.

1. In which region of the United States is California located?
   - Ⓐ Midwest
   - Ⓑ West
   - Ⓒ Southwest
   - Ⓓ Southeast

2. Which of the following describes a reason why the population of the Sunbelt increased after World War II?
   - Ⓐ Many businesses came to take advantage of the warm climate, natural resources, and lower wages.
   - Ⓑ Many businesses came to take advantage of the warm climate, natural resources, and higher wages.
   - Ⓒ Many businesses came to take advantage of the cool climate, renewable resources, and lower wages.
   - Ⓓ Many businesses came to take advantage of the cool climate, natural resources, and higher wages.

3. Where have most immigrants to the United States come from since the late 1900s?
   - Ⓐ Europe or Latin America
   - Ⓑ Europe or Africa
   - Ⓒ Asia or Latin America
   - Ⓓ Asia or Africa

4. Which statement describes a republic?
   - Ⓐ People elect representatives to make laws and run the government.
   - Ⓑ People elect a President to make laws and run the government.
   - Ⓒ The President appoints representatives to make laws and run the government.
   - Ⓓ Each individual has the opportunity to vote on every decision the government makes.

5. Responsibilities of citizenship include all of the following EXCEPT
   - Ⓐ obeying the law
   - Ⓑ serving on juries
   - Ⓒ paying taxes
   - Ⓓ making laws

6. Which statement is true about the system that is used to elect the President of the United States?
   - Ⓐ The presidential candidate who gets a majority of the vote wins the election.
   - Ⓑ For most states, the presidential candidate who gets a majority of the vote in a state gets all of that state's electoral votes.
   - Ⓒ The two presidential candidates who get a majority of the vote are accepted to the electoral college.
   - Ⓓ Citizens in each city vote for electors to decide who will become President.

7. How do consumers benefit from supply and demand?
   (A) If the supply and the demand are both high, prices will increase.
   (B) If the supply and the demand are both low, prices will increase.
   (C) If the supply is high and the demand is low, prices will decrease.
   (D) If the supply is low and the demand is high, prices will decrease.

8. What became the two fastest-growing areas for jobs in the late 1900s and early 2000s?
   (A) education and social services
   (B) computers and health care
   (C) space technology and government
   (D) media and environmental science

9. What is the purpose of the North American Free Trade Agreement?
   (A) to discourage trade between North American countries and the rest of the world
   (B) to encourage trade between North American countries and the rest of the world
   (C) to discourage trade between the United States, Canada, and Mexico
   (D) to encourage trade between the United States, Canada, and Mexico

10. Which event did NOT occur on September 11, 2001?
    (A) Terrorists crashed two planes into the twin towers of the World Trade Center.
    (B) Terrorists crashed a plane into the Pentagon.
    (C) Terrorists crashed a plane into the White House.
    (D) A hijacked plane crashed in a field in Pennsylvania.

11. Why did the United States attack Taliban troops and al Qaeda training bases in Afghanistan?
    (A) The Taliban and al Qaeda had carried out several attacks in the past against American targets.
    (B) The Taliban and al Qaeda claimed responsibility for the attacks of September 11.
    (C) Al Qaeda refused to capture Osama bin Laden and other Taliban leaders.
    (D) The Taliban refused to capture Osama bin Laden and other al Qaeda leaders.

12. Why did the United States and Great Britain lead a coalition force into Iraq in 2003?
    (A) They wanted to remove Saddam Hussein from power.
    (B) They discovered weapons of mass destruction in Iraq.
    (C) Iraq invaded Kuwait and Saudi Arabia.
    (D) Osama bin Laden and other al Qaeda leaders were hiding in Iraq.

13. Which of the following might help
protect the environment in the future?
Ⓐ an increase in the use of coal
Ⓑ an increase of carbon dioxide
Ⓒ nuclear power
Ⓓ the hydrogen-fueled car

14. About how many deaths does malaria
cause each year?
Ⓐ one thousand
Ⓑ five thousand
Ⓒ two million
Ⓓ two billion

15. What are scientists at NASA working to
develop by the year 2014?
Ⓐ a machine with artificial intelligence
Ⓑ a computer chip to help people with
brain damage
Ⓒ a satellite that can take pictures
of Earth
Ⓓ a spacecraft that can travel to Mars
and bring samples back to Earth

Part 2: Skills Test

Directions: Use complete sentences to answer questions 1–5. Use a separate sheet
of paper if you need more space.

1. Read the passage. Write a sentence that is a generalization of the information in the
passage. **Make Generalizations**

> As a result of globalization, people today share more things than ever before.
> People all over the world can see the same movies and television shows, listen
> to the same music, and even dress alike. More and more people travel to
> foreign countries for both business and vacations.

_____

_____

2. Describe how Americans responded to the terrorist attacks of September 11, 2001.
Main Idea and Details

_____

_____

_____

_____

_____

3. Complete the chart below. Summarize the details about the global challenges facing people around the world. **Summarize**

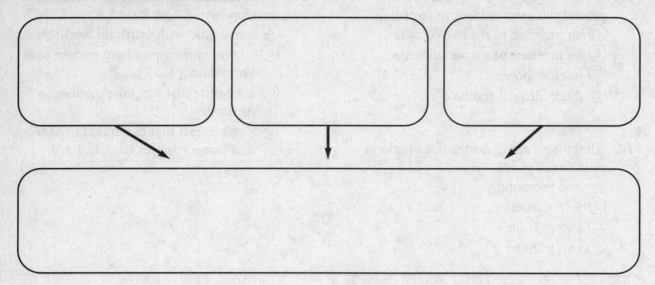

4. What are some benefits of using the Internet to research a topic? **Internet Research**

_____

_____

_____

_____

_____

5. What is population density? What does a population density map show?
Compare Population Density Maps

_____

_____

_____

Overview Test

Part 1: Content Test

Directions: Fill in the circle next to the correct answer.

Lesson Objective (1:1)

1. Many scholars think people first migrated to North America by
   - (A) boat.
   - ● crossing a land bridge between Asia and North America.
   - (C) walking north from South America.
   - (D) swimming from Caribbean islands.

Lesson Objective (1:2)

2. The first people to arrive in North America survived by
   - ● hunting.
   - (B) farming.
   - (C) trading.
   - (D) manufacturing.

Lesson Objective (1:2)

3. Native American cultures differed in part based on
   - (A) how long they had been living in North America.
   - (B) what part of Asia they came from.
   - (C) whether they preferred hunting or farming.
   - ● the resources available to them.

Lesson Objective (1:3)

4. Which of the following is NOT a result of the Columbian Exchange?
   - (A) Cattle and horses came from Europe to the Americas.
   - ● Columbus landed on some islands off the coast of North America.
   - (C) Crops such as potatoes and beans came to Europe from the Americas.
   - (D) Native Americans were exposed to European diseases.

Lesson Objective (2:1)

5. Which of the following is NOT one of the reasons Europeans came to the American colonies?
   - (A) religious freedom
   - (B) economic opportunity
   - (C) the chance to explore
   - ● the absence of a fur trade

Lesson Objective (2:2)

6. The Jamestown colony is remembered mainly because
   - ● it was the first permanent English colony in North America.
   - (B) it was a major East Coast Spanish colony.
   - (C) the first Thanksgiving was held there.
   - (D) Squanto helped the Pilgrims there survive.

Lesson Objective (2:3)

7. Plantations were most common in the Southern Colonies because
   - (A) most African Americans lived there.
   - ● the soil and climate were suitable to plantation agriculture.
   - (C) southern farmers did not like growing wheat.
   - (D) the South lacked ports for a fishing industry.

Lesson Objective (2:3)

8. Which of the following were NOT factors in the early colonial economy of New England?
   - (A) plentiful supply of wood
   - (B) rich fishing grounds
   - ● warm weather for plantations
   - (D) shipping industry

Lesson Objective (3:1)

9. Why were many colonists angered by the Stamp Act?
   - (A) They thought the tax was too high.
   - (B) They thought the tax was too low.
   - (C) They had already declared independence from Great Britain.
   - ● They did not think the British government had the right to tax them.

Lesson Objective (3:2)

10. Which of the following was NOT a key event of the American Revolution?
    - (A) Declaration of Independence
    - (B) Battle of Saratoga
    - (C) Battle of Yorktown
    - ● the Constitutional Convention

Lesson Objective (3:3)

11. Which of the following is NOT a key feature of the United States government under the Constitution?
    - ● established by the Articles of Confederation
    - (B) includes checks and balances
    - (C) is a republic
    - (D) includes the Bill of Rights

Lesson Objective (4:1)

12. Disagreement between members of George Washington's Cabinet helped lead the development of
    - (A) Washington, D.C.
    - (B) a strong national government.
    - ● political parties.
    - (D) the executive branch.

Lesson Objective (4:2)

13. The Louisiana Purchase
    - (A) belonged to Sacagawea.
    - ● doubled the size of the United States.
    - (C) was never explored.
    - (D) led to war with France.

Lesson Objective (4:3)

14. The great change in the way goods were manufactured that took place in the early decades of United States history is known as the
    - ● Industrial Revolution.
    - (B) Monroe Doctrine.
    - (C) cotton gin.
    - (D) Report on Manufactures.

Lesson Objective (4:4)

15. The abolitionists favored
    - (A) manifest destiny.
    - (B) war with Mexico.
    - ● an end to slavery.
    - (D) territorial expansion of the United States.

Part 2: Skills Test

Directions: Use complete sentences to answer questions 1–5. Use a separate sheet of paper if you need more space.

1. Describe how scholars think the first humans arrived in North America and developed into different Native American groups. **Summarize**

   Native Americans may have crossed a land bridge between Asia and North America. As they spread across North America, they changed their way of life based on the available resources. This helped different Native American cultures emerge.

2. What was the effect of the creation of the House of Burgesses in Virginia? **Cause and Effect**

   The development of the House of Burgesses helped colonists establish the idea of self-government in the colonies.

3. What can you conclude about the abolitionists and their feelings about slavery? **Draw Conclusions**

   The abolitionists believed slavery was wrong and should be eliminated.

4. Complete the chart below by summarizing the details about events in the British colonies. **Summarize**

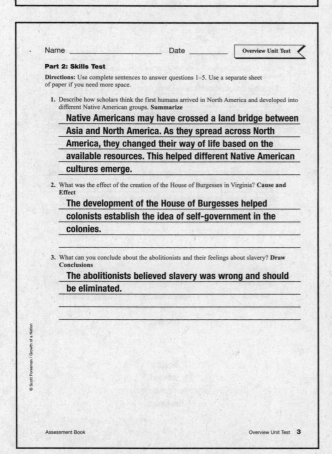

Stamp Act angers colonists.

Patriot leaders meet in Philadelphia.

British soldiers fire on Boston protesters.

Patriots and British fight at Lexington and Concord.

Relations between Great Britain and the colonies worsened in the 1760s and early 1770s, leading the colonists to declare their independence.

5. Look at the map below. If you wanted to find how to drive from one city in Virginia to another, would you seek a larger-scale map or a smaller-scale map? **Compare Maps at Different Scales**

   You would seek a small-scale map that would provide information about the entire state.

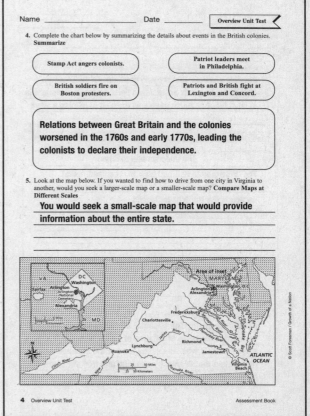

Chapter 1 Test

Part 1: Content Test

Directions: Fill in the circle next to the correct answer.

Lesson Objective (1:1)

1. Where did most Southerners live by the mid-1850s?
   Ⓐ cities and large towns
   Ⓑ cities and plantations
   ● farms and small towns
   Ⓓ farms and plantations

Lesson Objective (1:1)

2. In what region of the United States were most of the nation's cities located by the 1850s?
   ● North
   Ⓑ South
   Ⓒ East
   Ⓓ West

Lesson Objective (1:3)

3. What was the North's point of view on slavery by the 1850s?
   ● Most Northern states had outlawed slavery.
   Ⓑ Most Northern states supported slavery.
   Ⓒ Most Northern factories hired slaves for workers.
   Ⓓ Slaves were found only on farms in the North.

Lesson Objective (1:2)

4. Which of the following describes slavery's role in the Southern economy?
   Ⓐ Slavery was expensive.
   Ⓑ Slavery was forbidden.
   Ⓒ Slavery was a luxury.
   ● Slavery was profitable.

Lesson Objective (2:1)

5. Which of the following is one way in which slaves resisted slavery?
   Ⓐ telling family stories
   Ⓑ meeting with owners
   Ⓒ singing in the fields
   ● holding back on work

Lesson Objective (2:2)

6. Which of the following was a slave rebellion that ended in the slaves returning to Africa?
   Ⓐ New Haven rebellion
   ● *Amistad* rebellion
   Ⓒ slave rebellion
   Ⓓ abolitionists' rebellion

Lesson Objective (2:3)

7. What means did Harriet Tubman and others use to help slaves reach freedom in the North?
   ● Underground Railroad
   Ⓑ churches
   Ⓒ schools
   Ⓓ *Amistad* rebellion

Lesson Objective (2:4)

8. Which of the following describes the lifestyle of free African Americans?
   ● They lived in fear of losing their freedom.
   Ⓑ They lived the same as white citizens.
   Ⓒ They lived as paid slaves.
   Ⓓ They received many benefits.

Lesson Objective (3:1)

9. What problem did the Missouri Compromise solve?
   Ⓐ Southern states wanted to admit a free state.
   ● Northerners did not want more slave states than free states.
   Ⓒ Missouri had to choose to be a free state or a slave state.
   Ⓓ Missouri wanted to join the United States as a free state.

Lesson Objective (3:2)

10. What led to violence in Kansas in 1854?
    ● Northerners and Southerners disagreed over the results of the slavery vote.
    Ⓑ People voted for Kansas to be a slave state.
    Ⓒ People voted for Kansas to be a free state.
    Ⓓ Nebraska was split into Kansas and Nebraska.

Lesson Objective (3:3)

11. Why were people outraged at the Supreme Court's decision in the Dred Scott case?
    Ⓐ They believed it would solve many problems.
    Ⓑ They agreed with the decision.
    ● The Court said African Americans had no rights.
    Ⓓ The Court ruled in favor of Scott.

Lesson Objective (3:4)

12. Which statement represents Lincoln's and Douglas's views on slavery?
    Ⓐ They agreed on slavery.
    Ⓑ Neither one cared about slavery.
    Ⓒ Douglas opposed slavery, but Lincoln believed slavery had its place.
    ● Lincoln opposed slavery, but Douglas thought slavery had its place.

Lesson Objective (4:1)

13. Which of the following is a reason Southern states seceded from the Union?
    Ⓐ They wanted to support the Union.
    Ⓑ They wanted to abolish slavery.
    Ⓒ They wanted their own flag.
    ● They wanted to keep slavery.

Lesson Objective (4:2)

14. What officially started the Civil War?
    ● battle at Fort Sumter
    Ⓑ disagreements between the North and the South
    Ⓒ disagreements between Lincoln and Davis
    Ⓓ disagreements between abolitionists and slave owners

Lesson Objective (4:3)

15. What did the North hope to achieve by fighting the Civil War?
    Ⓐ preservation of states' rights
    ● an end to slavery
    Ⓒ equality for all
    Ⓓ preservation of the slave system

Part 2: Skills Test

Directions: Use complete sentences to answer questions 1–5. Use a separate sheet of paper if you need more space.

1. Why did Southern states fear the outlawing of slavery? **Main Idea and Details**

   Possible answers: Slavery was profitable to the Southern economy. The goods an enslaved person produced brought in at least twice as much money as the cost of owning a slave.

2. In the chart below, give details that explain how the Underground Railroad was able to be so successful in its fight against slavery. **Main Idea and Details**

The Underground Railroad
The Underground Railroad was an organized, secret system. Both whites and African Americans helped slaves escape to the North or to Canada.

3. What was the underlying issue the Missouri Compromise was intended to address? Was it successful or not? **Draw Conclusions**

   Possible answers: The Missouri Compromise was intended to address the issue of balance of power between free and slave states; it was successful for a while because it maintained the balance by allowing one free state and one slave state to join the Union at the same time.

4. Why do you think Jefferson Davis thought it was important to capture Fort Sumter? **Hypothesize**

   Possible answer: Jefferson Davis knew that the Northern forces would be a "powerful opposition" to the Confederacy. The Confederacy had already taken control of most forts and military property in the South, but Fort Sumter was still under Union control and could be used as a threat.

5. Complete the chart below. List some of the goals people in the United States had as they entered into the Civil War. **Main Idea and Details**

   Possible answer: People fought hoping to achieve different goals. In the Civil War some people were fighting to end slavery, some to preserve slavery, and some to preserve the Union.

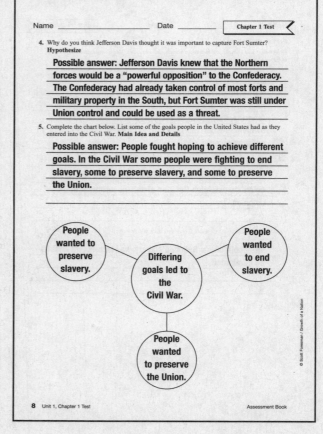

People wanted to preserve slavery.

Differing goals led to the Civil War.

People wanted to end slavery.

People wanted to preserve the Union.

Chapter 2 Test

Part 1: Content Test

Directions: Fill in the circle next to the correct answer.

Lesson Objective (1:1)

1. Which of the following did the South see as its advantage in the war?
   - Ⓐ The South had plenty of cotton for cloth.
   - Ⓑ The South produced more than half of the country's wheat.
   - Ⓒ The army needed supplies.
   - ● Southerners' rural lifestyles better prepared soldiers for war.

Lesson Objective (1:2)

2. Which of the following was a war strategy used by the Union?
   - Ⓐ stampede
   - ● blockade
   - Ⓒ bombing
   - Ⓓ air raid

Lesson Objective (1:2)

3. Which of the following did Confederates believe?
   - Ⓐ Northerners would fight a long time.
   - Ⓑ Britain would help the Union.
   - ● Northerners would grow tired of fighting and give up.
   - Ⓓ The Union would use the Anaconda Plan.

Lesson Objective (1:3)

4. Which of the following describes the early battles of the Civil War?
   - ● They were confusing because most of the troops were new to war.
   - Ⓑ They were well organized and efficient.
   - Ⓒ The Union always won because the North had better soldiers.
   - Ⓓ The Confederacy always won because the South had better soldiers.

Lesson Objective (1:4)

5. Which of the following describes the effect of new military technology on the Civil War?
   - Ⓐ More accurate weapons resulted in fewer casualties.
   - ● More accurate weapons resulted in many casualties.
   - Ⓒ Stronger ships resulted in fewer sea battles.
   - Ⓓ New weapons reduced the need for blockades.

Lesson Objective (2:1)

6. Which of the following was NOT experienced by both Northern and Southern soldiers?
   - Ⓐ Soldiers were unhappy with the food.
   - Ⓑ Soldiers saw friends die.
   - ● Soldiers often had to fight in bare feet.
   - Ⓓ Soldiers were drafted.

Lesson Objective (2:2)

7. What was the Emancipation Proclamation?
   - Ⓐ a statement giving freedom to all women
   - Ⓑ a statement giving freedom to all people in the United States
   - Ⓒ a statement giving freedom to all Confederate states still at war with the Union
   - ● a statement giving freedom to slaves in all Confederate states still at war with the Union

---

Lesson Objective (2:3)

8. What is one way African Americans served the Union's war effort?
   - ● They engaged in combat.
   - Ⓑ They protested against slavery.
   - Ⓒ They supported freedom and went to Canada.
   - Ⓓ They staged demonstrations to end the war.

Lesson Objective (2:4)

9. Which is NOT one way women contributed to the war effort?
   - Ⓐ They cared for the soldiers.
   - ● They ran the government.
   - Ⓒ They ran businesses.
   - Ⓓ They were spies.

Lesson Objective (3:1)

10. Which of the following describes the Battle of Gettysburg?
    - Ⓐ Lee and Pickett battled against each other, and the North won.
    - Ⓑ Lee's retreat to Virginia won the battle for the South.
    - Ⓒ The Pennsylvania battle was won by the South.
    - ● The three-day struggle was won by the North.

Lesson Objective (3:3)

11. Which cut the Confederacy in two?
    - ● Battle of Vicksburg
    - Ⓑ Battle of Gettysburg
    - Ⓒ Battle of Savannah
    - Ⓓ Battle of Bull Run

Lesson Objective (3:4)

12. Which is a result of total war?
    - Ⓐ Everybody helps out any way they can.
    - Ⓑ An area is squeezed the way a snake would squeeze its prey.
    - Ⓒ Supplies are cut off.
    - ● The people's will to fight is destroyed.

Lesson Objective (4:1)

13. Why did Congress disagree with President Andrew Johnson's Reconstruction plan?
    - ● They thought it was too easy on the South.
    - Ⓑ They did not want to include all of the Southern states.
    - Ⓒ They did not want to allow all African Americans to be free.
    - Ⓓ They thought the plan was cruel to Southerners.

Lesson Objective (4:2)

14. Which of the following was an effect of the Reconstruction Acts?
    - Ⓐ All African Americans had the right to vote.
    - ● African American men had the right to vote.
    - Ⓒ African Americans could lobby Congress for the right to vote.
    - Ⓓ African Americans were not allowed to vote.

Lesson Objective (4:3)

15. What did the passage of the Thirteenth, Fourteenth, and Fifteenth Amendments mean for African Americans?
    - ● African Americans were free citizens, and the men could vote.
    - Ⓑ African Americans became citizens.
    - Ⓒ Slavery was abolished.
    - Ⓓ Equal protection could not be denied any citizen.

Part 2: Skills Test

Directions: Use complete sentences to answer questions 1–5. Use a separate sheet of paper if you need more space.

1. How did the South plan to win the war? **Summarize**

   Southerners planned to wear down the North because they believed that Northerners would quickly grow tired of fighting and give up. They also were hoping to get aid from Britain.

2. Support the statement in the box below with details. **Main Idea and Details**

   Life was difficult for soldiers during the Civil War.

   Detail 1

   Supplies were short, and soldiers had to make do with food they disliked.

   Detail 2

   They had to walk long distances and often wore out their shoes.

   Detail 3

   They were exposed to harsh weather conditions with no protection.

   Detail 4

   They suffered and died from disease and infection.

---

3. Why do you think General Grant allowed total war to be used to defeat Lee but then offered to feed Lee's men after their surrender? **Draw Conclusions**

   Possible answer: Grant did what was necessary to win the war. However, he realized that the Confederate soldiers were again his countrymen and that everyone would have to forgive each other for the nation to heal.

4. Why did Reconstruction include the Thirteenth, Fourteenth, and Fifteenth Amendments? **Make Inferences**

   Possible answer: The goal of Reconstruction was to rebuild and heal the nation. Abolishing slavery was the first step in recognizing African Americans as valuable people. Granting citizenship and the right to vote helped make all men equal.

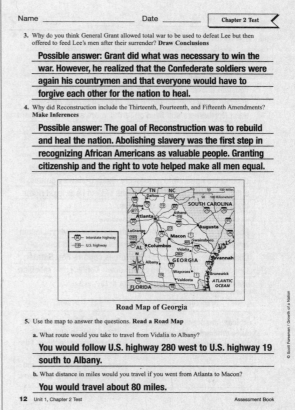

Road Map of Georgia

5. Use the map to answer the questions. **Read a Road Map**

   a. What route would you take to travel from Vidalia to Albany?

   You would follow U.S. highway 280 west to U.S. highway 19 south to Albany.

   b. What distance in miles would you travel if you went from Atlanta to Macon?

   You would travel about 80 miles.

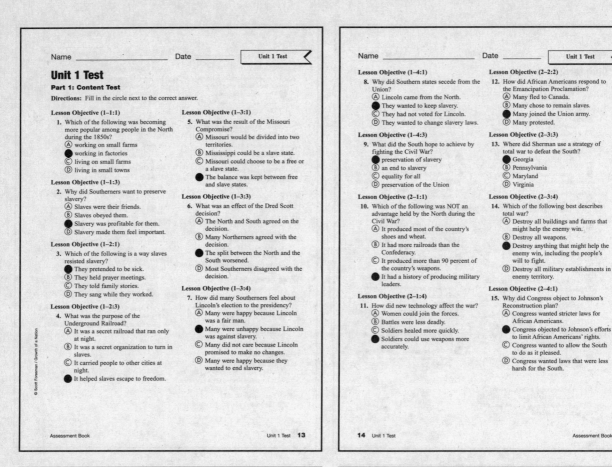

Unit 1 Test

Part 1: Content Test

Directions: Fill in the circle next to the correct answer.

Lesson Objective (1–1:1)

1. Which of the following was becoming more popular among people in the North during the 1850s?
   (A) working on small farms
   ● working in factories
   (C) living on small farms
   (D) living in small towns

Lesson Objective (1–1:3)

2. Why did Southerners want to preserve slavery?
   (A) Slaves were their friends.
   (B) Slaves obeyed them.
   ● Slavery was profitable for them.
   (D) Slavery made them feel important.

Lesson Objective (1–2:1)

3. Which of the following is a way slaves resisted slavery?
   ● They pretended to be sick.
   (B) They held prayer meetings.
   (C) They told family stories.
   (D) They sang while they worked.

Lesson Objective (1–2:3)

4. What was the purpose of the Underground Railroad?
   (A) It was a secret railroad that ran only at night.
   (B) It was a secret organization to turn in slaves.
   (C) It carried people to other cities at night.
   ● It helped slaves escape to freedom.

Lesson Objective (1–3:1)

5. What was the result of the Missouri Compromise?
   (A) Missouri would be divided into two territories.
   (B) Mississippi could be a slave state.
   (C) Missouri could choose to be a free or a slave state.
   ● The balance was kept between free and slave states.

Lesson Objective (1–3:3)

6. What was NOT an effect of the Dred Scott decision?
   (A) The North and South agreed on the decision.
   (B) Many Northerners agreed with the decision.
   ● The split between the North and the South worsened.
   (D) Most Southerners disagreed with the decision.

Lesson Objective (1–3:4)

7. How did many Southerners feel about Lincoln's election to the presidency?
   (A) Many were happy because Lincoln was a fair man.
   ● Many were unhappy because Lincoln was against slavery.
   (C) Many did not care because Lincoln promised to make no changes.
   (D) Many were happy because they wanted to end slavery.

Lesson Objective (1–4:1)

8. Why did Southern states secede from the Union?
   (A) Lincoln came from the North.
   ● They wanted to keep slavery.
   (C) They had not voted for Lincoln.
   (D) They wanted to change slavery laws.

Lesson Objective (1–4:3)

9. What did the South hope to achieve by fighting the Civil War?
   ● preservation of slavery
   (B) an end to slavery
   (C) equality for all
   (D) preservation of the Union

Lesson Objective (2–1:1)

10. Which of the following was NOT an advantage held by the North during the Civil War?
    (A) It produced most of the country's shoes and wheat.
    (B) It had more railroads than the Confederacy.
    (C) It produced more than 90 percent of the country's weapons.
    ● It had a history of producing military leaders.

Lesson Objective (2–1:4)

11. How did new technology affect the war?
    (A) Women could join the forces.
    (B) Battles were less deadly.
    (C) Soldiers healed more quickly.
    ● Soldiers could use weapons more accurately.

Lesson Objective (2–2:2)

12. How did African Americans respond to the Emancipation Proclamation?
    (A) Many fled to Canada.
    (B) Many chose to remain slaves.
    ● Many joined the Union army.
    (D) Many protested.

Lesson Objective (2–3:3)

13. Where did Sherman use a strategy of total war to defeat the South?
    ● Georgia
    (B) Pennsylvania
    (C) Maryland
    (D) Virginia

Lesson Objective (2–3:4)

14. Which of the following best describes total war?
    (A) Destroy all buildings and farms that might help the enemy win.
    (B) Destroy all weapons.
    ● Destroy anything that might help the enemy win, including the people's will to fight.
    (D) Destroy all military establishments in enemy territory.

Lesson Objective (2–4:1)

15. Why did Congress object to Johnson's Reconstruction plan?
    (A) Congress wanted stricter laws for African Americans.
    ● Congress objected to Johnson's efforts to limit African Americans' rights.
    (C) Congress wanted to allow the South to do as it pleased.
    (D) Congress wanted laws that were less harsh for the South.

Part 2: Skills Test

Directions: Use complete sentences to answer questions 1–5. Use a separate sheet of paper if you need more space.

1. How did lifestyles in the North and the South differ during the mid-1800s? **Compare and Contrast**

   Possible answer: In the South, most people had a rural lifestyle. They lived on farms and in small towns. Although most Northerners still lived on farms, more and more of them worked in factories and lived in large towns and cities. They had an urban lifestyle.

2. What do you think were two long-term effects of the Dred Scott decision? **Draw Conclusions**

   Accept all reasonable answers. Possible answers: It firmly divided the nation into antislavery and pro-slavery groups; it established that African Americans did not have legal rights that were equal to those of whites.

3. What steps led to the outbreak of the Civil War? **Sequence**

   Possible answer: North and South split over slavery; Lincoln is elected President; Southern states secede and form Confederacy; Jefferson Davis's forces capture Fort Sumter; Lincoln uses Union forces to put down Confederate rebellion.

4. Complete the chart below. Support the main idea in the box with details.
   Main Idea and Details

Main Idea	Details
African Americans' lives were different at the end of Reconstruction.	New laws were passed that placed African Americans under many restrictions. Life became very difficult for most. Work was scarce, and many became sharecroppers.

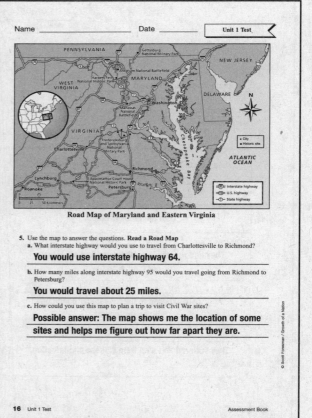

Road Map of Maryland and Eastern Virginia

5. Use the map to answer the questions. **Read a Road Map**
   a. What interstate highway would you use to travel from Charlottesville to Richmond?
      You would use interstate highway 64.
   b. How many miles along interstate highway 95 would you travel going from Richmond to Petersburg?
      You would travel about 25 miles.
   c. How could you use this map to plan a trip to visit Civil War sites?
      Possible answer: The map shows me the location of some sites and helps me figure out how far apart they are.

Chapter 3 Test
Part 1: Content Test
Directions: Fill in the circle next to the correct answer.

Lesson Objective (1:1)
1. Which innovation used electricity to send news across the country?
   - Ⓐ the transcontinental railroad
   - Ⓑ the Pony Express
   - ● the telegraph
   - Ⓓ the stagecoach

Lesson Objective (1:2)
2. Which of the following best describes a major challenge faced by the Union Pacific railroad?
   - ● conflict with Native Americans
   - Ⓑ conflict with Chinese immigrants
   - Ⓒ competition among other railroad companies
   - Ⓓ the steep slopes of the Sierra Nevada

Lesson Objective (1:3)
3. Which group made up the largest part of the Central Pacific's workforce?
   - Ⓐ Irish immigrants
   - ● Chinese immigrants
   - Ⓒ African Americans
   - Ⓓ former Union Army soldiers

Lesson Objective (1:4)
4. Which innovation allowed people and goods to travel across the country in just a week?
   - Ⓐ the stagecoach
   - Ⓑ the Pony Express
   - ● the transcontinental railroad
   - Ⓓ the Morse Code

Lesson Objective (2:1)
5. What was the main purpose of the Homestead Act?
   - Ⓐ to bring an end to cattle drives
   - ● to encourage settlement on the Great Plains
   - Ⓒ to defeat the Native Americans
   - Ⓓ to provide a market for steel plows

Lesson Objective (2:2)
6. Which of the following was NOT one of the challenges typically faced by homesteaders?
   - ● high cost of land
   - Ⓑ harsh weather
   - Ⓒ large amount of grasshoppers
   - Ⓓ thick sod

Lesson Objective (2:3)
7. Why did many exodusters come to the Great Plains?
   - Ⓐ European immigrants forced them from their homes in the East.
   - Ⓑ They wanted to hunt buffalo.
   - ● They faced discrimination and lack of opportunity in the East.
   - Ⓓ They were seeking religious freedom.

Lesson Objective (2:4)
8. Which of the following was NOT a way that technology helped pioneers turn the Great Plains into productive farmland?
   - Ⓐ Stronger steel plows were used on the thick grasslands.
   - Ⓑ Windmills were used to pump water to the land's surface.
   - Ⓒ Barbed wire was used to keep animals away from crops.
   - ● Sod was used as a building material to keep out bugs.

Lesson Objective (3:1)
9. Why were cattle drives profitable for Texas ranchers?
   - Ⓐ Cattle grew fatter as they traveled the trails.
   - Ⓑ People paid to watch the cattle drives.
   - ● Cattle could be sold for more money in the East.
   - Ⓓ Railroads paid ranchers to use their services.

Lesson Objective (3:2)
10. Which of the following best describes a reason why cattle drives came to an end?
   - Ⓐ Thousands of cattle ranchers moved west in search of gold.
   - Ⓑ Consumers became more interested in gold than cattle.
   - Ⓒ Farmers on the Great Plains began raising cattle.
   - ● They were no longer necessary once railroads reached Texas.

Lesson Objective (3:3)
11. Which of the following describes a lasting effect of the search for gold?
   - ● The quest for gold lured many settlers to the West.
   - Ⓑ Gold rushes left the West deserted with ghost towns.
   - Ⓒ Dreams of finding gold continue to attract many settlers each year.
   - Ⓓ Few miners actually found gold nuggets.

Lesson Objective (4:1)
12. Which of the following was NOT a change that threatened the way of life for Native Americans of the Great Plains?
   - Ⓐ decline in buffalo herds
   - ● widespread European diseases
   - Ⓒ spreading telegraph and railroad lines
   - Ⓓ arrival of miners, farmers, and ranchers

Lesson Objective (4:2)
13. Why is the Battle of Little Bighorn also known as "Custer's Last Stand"?
   - Ⓐ Custer resigned after witnessing the brutal Lakota defeat.
   - Ⓑ Custer was seriously injured as he led his forces to victory.
   - ● Custer was killed along with his entire forces.
   - Ⓓ Custer surrendered after his forces were surrounded by the Lakota.

Lesson Objective (4:2)
14. Which of the following describes the significance of the Battle of Wounded Knee?
   - Ⓐ It was the biggest victory Native Americans ever won over United States forces.
   - ● It was the last major battle between the United States and Native Americans.
   - Ⓒ It convinced the United States government to take stronger action against the Lakota and other Native American groups.
   - Ⓓ It allowed Native Americans to return to their traditional homelands.

Lesson Objective (4:3)
15. Which of the following is NOT an example of how Native American groups are keeping traditions alive today?
   - Ⓐ gaining control of more land
   - Ⓑ maintaining tribal languages
   - Ⓒ sharing tribal stories
   - ● launching raids on United States military sites

Part 2: Skills Test
Directions: Use complete sentences to answer questions 1–5. Use a separate sheet of paper if you need more space.

1. Write the following events about transportation and communication in the order in which they happened. **Sequence**

   The first telegraph line across the country was completed.

   A new business called the Pony Express began delivering mail from Missouri to California in just 10 days.

   The tracks of the Union Pacific and Central Pacific met at Promontory Point, Utah.

   Samuel Morse developed a method of sending messages along wires.

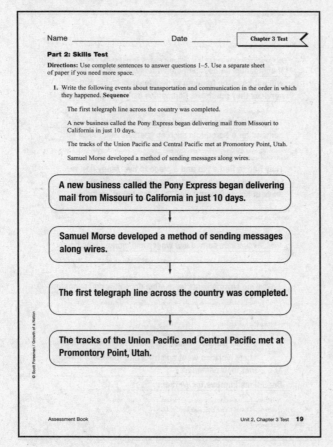

> **A new business called the Pony Express began delivering mail from Missouri to California in just 10 days.**
>
> ↓
>
> **Samuel Morse developed a method of sending messages along wires.**
>
> ↓
>
> **The first telegraph line across the country was completed.**
>
> ↓
>
> **The tracks of the Union Pacific and Central Pacific met at Promontory Point, Utah.**

2. Use details from the chapter to support the following statement. **Main Idea and Details**

   Gold rushes of the mid-1800s had lasting effects in the West.

   Possible answer: The hope of finding gold drew thousands of settlers to the West. Supply stations for miners grew into important cities. Growing towns offered opportunities for entrepreneurs.

3. What can you infer from the fact that the United States government forced many Native Americans of the Great Plains to move to reservations in the late 1800s? **Make Inferences**

   Possible answer: The United States government wanted the region to be open for expanding railroad lines, growing farms and ranches, and new towns.

4. What effect did the Battle of Little Bighorn have on Native Americans? **Cause and Effect**

   It convinced the United States government to take stronger action against Native Americans and led to the end of freedom for Native Americans of the Great Plains.

5. Study the climograph below. What generalization can you make about precipitation in Burlington, Vermont? **Read Climographs**

   Precipitation is consistent throughout the year, although it is heaviest in the summer months.

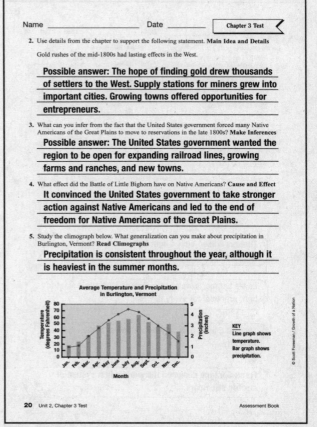

Average Temperature and Precipitation in Burlington, Vermont

KEY
Line graph shows temperature.
Bar graph shows precipitation.

Chapter 4 Test

Part 1: Content Test

Directions: Fill in the circle next to the correct answer.

Lesson Objective (1:1)

1. Who invented the telephone?
   - ● Alexander Graham Bell
   - Ⓑ Lewis Latimer
   - Ⓒ Frank Sprague
   - Ⓓ Frank Duryea

Lesson Objective (1:1)

2. Which of the following did Thomas Edison invent?
   - Ⓐ the airplane
   - Ⓑ the electric streetcar
   - ● the phonograph
   - Ⓓ the gasoline engine

Lesson Objective (1:2)

3. Which of the following represents an invention that changed transportation at the turn of the twentieth century?
   - Ⓐ the wagon
   - Ⓑ the Pony Express
   - ● the electric streetcar
   - Ⓓ the stagecoach

Lesson Objective (1:3)

4. Which of the following is NOT an example of how inventions of the late 1800s and early 1900s led to the rise of new industries?
   - Ⓐ Companies all over the country began selling and designing cars.
   - Ⓑ People started businesses to offer telephone service.
   - ● Airplane manufacturing became the country's leading industry.
   - Ⓓ Entrepreneurs built power stations to bring electricity to cities.

Lesson Objective (2:1)

5. Andrew Carnegie is known for which of the following?
   - Ⓐ inventing a new method for making steel
   - ● building a huge steel empire
   - Ⓒ building oil refineries
   - Ⓓ forming the Westinghouse Electric Company

Lesson Objective (2:1)

6. Which business leader founded Standard Oil Company?
   - Ⓐ Edwin Drake
   - ● John D. Rockefeller
   - Ⓒ William Randolph Hearst
   - Ⓓ Madame C. J. Walker

Lesson Objective (2:2)

7. Which of the following best describes how railroads helped the United States economy grow?
   - Ⓐ They charged high rates to farmers.
   - Ⓑ They used many tons of steel.
   - Ⓒ They helped end the shipping industry.
   - ● They helped businesses reach distant markets.

Lesson Objective (2:3)

8. Which of the following describes a free enterprise system?
   - Ⓐ Consumers have few choices about where they can buy goods and services.
   - Ⓑ Competition rarely exists among business owners.
   - Ⓒ The government regulates what business owners can produce and how much they can charge for products and services.
   - ● Business owners can decide what to produce and how much to charge for products or services.

Lesson Objective (2:4)

9. The growth of big business led to all EXCEPT which of the following?
   - Ⓐ By 1900, more Americans worked in factories than on farms.
   - ● People moved by the millions to rural areas.
   - Ⓒ Big business created millions of jobs.
   - Ⓓ The United States became the world's leading producer of manufactured goods.

Lesson Objective (3:1)

10. Which of the following is one of the main reasons immigrants came to the United States in the late 1800s and early 1900s?
    - Ⓐ They did not want religious freedom.
    - ● They hoped for economic opportunity.
    - Ⓒ They faced a lack of prejudice.
    - Ⓓ They wanted to live more simply.

Lesson Objective (3:2)

11. Angel Island differed from Ellis Island in that
    - Ⓐ it was the main immigrant station for European immigrants.
    - ● it was the main immigrant station for Chinese immigrants.
    - Ⓒ Angel Island was located on the East Coast.
    - Ⓓ most people stopped there for only a few hours.

Lesson Objective (3:3)

12. Immigrants often lived in communities with others from their home country because
    - Ⓐ it was illegal for them to live elsewhere.
    - Ⓑ they had no interest in building new lives in the United States.
    - ● it was a way to help make the adjustment to the United States easier.
    - Ⓓ housing was not available in other areas.

Lesson Objective (4:1)

13. Which of the following was NOT a contributing factor that led to the rise of labor unions?
    - Ⓐ Many workers earned low wages and worked long hours.
    - ● Many business owners were going on strike.
    - Ⓒ Working conditions were often unhealthy and dangerous.
    - Ⓓ Many workers labored in hot, cramped workshops.

Lesson Objective (4:2)

14. Which of the following was NOT a main goal of the American Federation of Labor?
    - Ⓐ safer working conditions
    - Ⓑ end child labor
    - Ⓒ better wages
    - ● a 12-hour workday

Lesson Objective (4:3)

15. Which of the following events shows how conditions improved for workers in the early 1900s?
    - Ⓐ the Homestead strike
    - Ⓑ the Triangle Shirtwaist fire
    - Ⓒ the completion of the transcontinental railroad
    - ● the establishment of Labor Day

Part 2: Skills Test

Directions: Use complete sentences to answer questions 1–5. Use a separate sheet of paper if you need more space.

1. Write the following events in the order in which they happened. **Sequence**

   Lewis Latimer developed a method that made electric light practical for every day use.

   Thomas Edison built an electric power station in New York City.

   Frank Sprague designed the world's first system of electric streetcars.

   Thomas Edison built a light bulb that glowed for two days.

   > Thomas Edison built a light bulb that glowed for two days.

   ↓

   > Lewis Latimer developed a method that made electric light practical for every day use.

   ↓

   > Thomas Edison built an electric power station in New York City.

   ↓

   > Frank Sprague designed the world's first system of electric streetcars.

2. Why do monopolies threaten the free enterprise system? **Draw Conclusions**

   If companies do not compete with each other, consumers will not have the freedom to decide what goods and services they purchase. Companies can keep prices high.

3. How did the growth of the automobile industry effect the oil industry? **Cause and Effect**

   The growth of the automobile industry created a huge demand for oil products such as gasoline and motor oil.

4. What challenges did many immigrants face once they gained entry into the United States? **Main Idea and Details**

   They had to find a job and a place to live. Many had to learn a new language and adjust to new traditions and ways of living. Others faced the hardship of prejudice.

5. Complete the outline by filling in the missing topics and details about the labor movement. **Write an Outline**

   The Labor Movement

   I. **Poor working Conditions**
      A. **Many workers earned low wages and worked long hours.**
         1. Steelworkers at Carnegie's Homestead Steel Works labored for 12 hours a day, seven days a week.
         2. Many children worked for just 10 to 20 cents a day.
      B. **Working environments were often unhealthy and dangerous.**
         1. Workers were trapped inside when a fire started at the Triangle Shirtwaist Company.

   II. **The Rise of Labor Unions**
      A. Workers joined together to fight for improved conditions.
         1. **Samuel Gompers formed the American Federation of Labor.**
         2. **Many workers went on strike until business owners met their demands.**

   III. **Conditions Improve for Workers**
      A. New laws shorten working hours and improve safety in the workplace.
      B. Congress declares Labor Day a national holiday.

© Scott Foresman / Growth of a Nation

Unit 2 Test

Part 1: Content Test

Directions: Fill in the circle next to the correct answer.

Lesson Objective (3–1:1)

1. Which of the following could deliver mail from Missouri to California in just 10 days?
   - Ⓐ the telegraph
   - Ⓑ the "horseless carriage"
   - ● the Pony Express
   - Ⓓ the stagecoach

Lesson Objective (3–1:2)

2. Which of the following describes a challenge faced by the Union Pacific railroad?
   - Ⓐ It had to build through the Sierra Nevada.
   - ● It faced conflict with Native Americans.
   - Ⓒ It faced conflict with Chinese immigrants.
   - Ⓓ The government did not support a transcontinental railroad.

Lesson Objective (3–2:2)

3. Which best describes a challenge facing homesteaders on the Great Plains?
   - Ⓐ They had to pay about $10 for 160 acres of land.
   - Ⓑ Land on the Great Plains was dry but very fertile.
   - Ⓒ They had to pass through miles of barbed wire.
   - ● They had to bust through sod before planting crops.

Lesson Objective (3–2:4)

4. Steel plows were especially important to Great Plains farmers because
   - Ⓐ there was a shortage of iron.
   - Ⓑ there was a shortage of farm animals to pull plows.
   - ● the sod was extremely thick on the Great Plains.
   - Ⓓ steel plows were less costly than iron ones.

Lesson Objective (3–3:2)

5. The arrival of railroads in Texas helped end the cattle drives because
   - ● they made it unnecessary to drive cattle to distant railroad centers.
   - Ⓑ the railroads blocked key cattle trails.
   - Ⓒ easterners could come to Texas to buy meat.
   - Ⓓ buffalo replaced cattle as a major meat source.

Lesson Objective (3–3:3)

6. Which of the following was NOT an effect of the search for gold in the West?
   - Ⓐ Supply stations for miners grew into important cities.
   - ● Gold rushes left the East deserted with ghost towns.
   - Ⓒ Dreams of finding gold attracted thousands of settlers.
   - Ⓓ Growing towns offered opportunities for entrepreneurs.

Lesson Objective (3–4:2)

7. The Battle of Little Bighorn convinced the United States that
   - Ⓐ it would not be able to defeat certain Native American groups.
   - Ⓑ the conflict would not be resolved until Native Americans could return to their traditional homelands.
   - Ⓒ moving Native American groups to reservations was not a good idea.
   - ● it should take stronger action against Native Americans.

Lesson Objective (4–1:1)

8. Which of the following did Thomas Edison invent?
   - ● a light bulb with a carbon filament
   - Ⓑ the typewriter
   - Ⓒ the radio
   - Ⓓ the automobile

Lesson Objective (4–1:2)

9. What do the electric street car and the "horseless carriage" have in common?
   - Ⓐ They were invented by Thomas Edison.
   - Ⓑ They were both outlawed at one time.
   - ● They changed transportation at the turn of the twentieth century.
   - Ⓓ They were outdated by the early 1900s.

Lesson Objective (4–2:1)

10. George Westinghouse is known for
    - Ⓐ his monopoly of the oil industry.
    - ● developing a new technology for delivering electricity.
    - Ⓒ controlling the banking industry.
    - Ⓓ building a steel empire.

Lesson Objective (4–2:4)

11. Which of the following is a result of the rise of big business in the late 1800s and early 1900s?
    - Ⓐ More people left the United States to live in other countries.
    - Ⓑ Many people moved from cities to rural areas.
    - ● The United States became the world's biggest producer of manufactured goods.
    - Ⓓ Many United States cities became ghost towns.

Lesson Objective (4–3:1)

12. Which of the following is NOT a reason why many immigrants came to the United States in the late 1800s and early 1900s?
    - Ⓐ to escape poverty
    - Ⓑ to escape hunger
    - ● they had many rights at home
    - Ⓓ they faced a lack of religious freedom at home

Lesson Objective (4–3:2)

13. What did Ellis Island and Angel Island share in common?
    - Ⓐ Both were located on the West Coast.
    - Ⓑ Both were located on the East Coast.
    - Ⓒ Both held immigrants until they could prove they had relatives living in the country.
    - ● Both were main immigration stations for immigrants arriving in the country.

Lesson Objective (4–4:1)

14. Which of the following describes the typical week of a steelworker at Carnegie's Homestead Steel Works?
    - Ⓐ five days a week, eight hours a day
    - Ⓑ five days a week, ten hours a day
    - Ⓒ seven days a week, four hours a day
    - ● seven days a week, twelve hours a day

Lesson Objective (4–4:2)

15. Which of the following best describes the main goals of labor unions such as the American Federation of Labor?
    - ● to get higher pay, shorter working hours, and safer working conditions
    - Ⓑ to hire new workers and start new holidays
    - Ⓒ to organize strikes and find new jobs
    - Ⓓ to pass child labor laws

Part 2: Skills Test

Directions: Use complete sentences to answer questions 1–5. Use a separate sheet of paper if you need more space.

1. Describe the changes that took place in transportation in the late 1800s.
   Main Idea and Details

   The growth of railroads allowed people to travel and transport goods more quickly. The transcontinental railroad allowed people to travel across the United States in just a week. Electric streetcars greatly improved urban transportation. The first cars were built in the 1890s.

2. What was the purpose of the Homestead Act? **Summarize**

   The purpose of the Homestead Act was to encourage settlers to move to the Great Plains.

3. What conditions led to the rise of labor unions in the late 1800s and early 1900s?
   Cause and Effect

   Many workers had to work for long hours and received low wages. Many had to work in hot, cramped workshops, and conditions were often unhealthy and dangerous. Many young children worked in unsafe conditions.

4. Write the following events in the order in which they happened. **Sequence**

   Crazy Horse led the Lakota to victory at the Battle of Little Bighorn.

   Gold was discovered in the Black Hills.

   The Lakota signed a treaty with the United States that created the Great Lakota Reservation.

   > The Lakota signed a treaty with the United States that created the Great Lakota Reservation.
   >
   > ↓
   >
   > Gold was discovered in the Black Hills.
   >
   > ↓
   >
   > Crazy Horse led the Lakota to victory at the Battle of Little Bighorn.

5. Look at the map below. What time is it in Boston when it is 4:00 P.M. in Los Angeles?
   Read a Time Zone Map

   It is 7:00 p.m. in Boston.

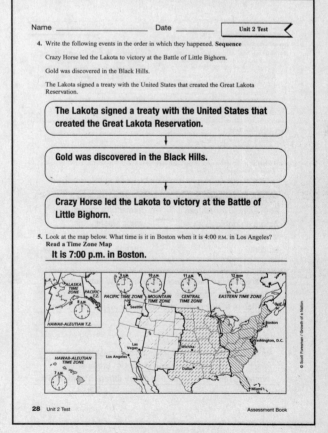

Chapter 5 Test
Part 1: Content Test
Directions: Fill in the circle next to the correct answer.

Lesson Objective (1:1)

1. How did the mechanization of farms change the lives of rural people in the 1800s and early 1900s?
   - Ⓐ It led them to grow fewer crops.
   - Ⓑ It increased the need for farm labor.
   - Ⓒ It forced farmers into deeper and deeper debt.
   - ● It led to larger farms that raised cash crops.

Lesson Objective (1:2)

2. Which is NOT an example of how industry in the late 1880s gave people greater access to all kinds of goods?
   - Ⓐ More goods were being invented and produced.
   - ● People on farms and ranches made almost everything they needed by hand.
   - Ⓒ Goods were less expensive to buy than ever before.
   - Ⓓ Stores increased in number, and mail-order businesses were established.

Lesson Objective (1:3)

3. In what way did telephones affect life in the 1800s?
   - ● People were pleased to be able to communicate without having to travel.
   - Ⓑ Most people no longer wanted or needed to use the mail system.
   - Ⓒ Alexander Graham Bell's company filled rural areas with telephone poles.
   - Ⓓ People protested against the sight of poles and lines.

Lesson Objective (1:4)

4. What was the main purpose of the Rural Electrification Act?
   - Ⓐ to encourage the use of wind and water power
   - Ⓑ to create streetcar systems in cities
   - ● to create and improve electric service in rural areas
   - Ⓓ to end people's need for electricity

Lesson Objective (2:1)

5. Which of the following was NOT a factor in the growth of cities in the late 1800s?
   - ● agricultural depression
   - Ⓑ mechanization of farms
   - Ⓒ immigration
   - Ⓓ urbanization

Lesson Objective (2:2)

6. What was one result of rapid industrialization and urbanization?
   - Ⓐ Most people in cities started living in large homes.
   - Ⓑ Factories moved away from residential areas.
   - Ⓒ People quit their city jobs and moved to the country.
   - ● Cities became overcrowded.

Lesson Objective (2:3)

7. Which is NOT one of the challenges faced by urban areas as a result of population and technological changes?
   - Ⓐ There was more garbage and waste.
   - Ⓑ The air became polluted.
   - ● Fewer workers were available for factory jobs.
   - Ⓓ Diseases spread quickly among people living close together.

Lesson Objective (2:4)

8. How did Jane Addams try to solve some of the problems faced by the city of Chicago?
   - Ⓐ She started schools for under-privileged city children.
   - ● She opened a settlement house to help immigrants and working families.
   - Ⓒ She wrote articles for the *New York Tribune* about the hardships faced by immigrants.
   - Ⓓ She was active in the YMCA.

Lesson Objective (3:1)

9. What is one thing that African Americans, Hispanic groups, Chinese immigrants, and Jews had in common in the late 1800s?
   - ● Many faced prejudice and segregation in different areas of their lives.
   - Ⓑ They ran for public office in great numbers and quickly gained political power.
   - Ⓒ Most moved away from cities to work on farms.
   - Ⓓ Many became leaders in the manufacturing industry and earned a great deal of money.

Lesson Objective (3:2)

10. What effect did the passage of Jim Crow laws in the 1880s have on the lives of African Americans?
    - Ⓐ It made racial segregation illegal in the United States.
    - ● It made racial segregation legal in the South.
    - Ⓒ It made better jobs available to African Americans.
    - Ⓓ It improved education for African American schoolchildren.

Lesson Objective (3:4)

11. Which of the following was NOT a factor in the Great Migration?
    - Ⓐ World War I
    - Ⓑ northern African American newspapers
    - Ⓒ encouragement of northern African Americans
    - ● total equality for African Americans in the North

Lesson Objective (3:5)

12. How did African American activist Booker T. Washington respond to discrimination and work toward equality?
    - Ⓐ He started an African American newspaper.
    - Ⓑ He became a scientist.
    - ● He founded the Tuskegee Institute, a college for African Americans.
    - Ⓓ He helped start the National Association for the Advancement of Colored People.

Lesson Objective (4:1)

13. What happened as a result of the women's suffrage movement?
    - Ⓐ Women were no longer allowed to do certain jobs in factories or on farms.
    - ● Congress passed the Nineteenth Amendment, which gave women the right to vote.
    - Ⓒ Women were allowed to enter the armed services.
    - Ⓓ New inventions made housework and farm work easier to do.

Lesson Objective (4:2)

14. Which is NOT an example of the new rights and educational opportunities gained for women in the 1800s?
    - ● Women could work on farms.
    - Ⓑ Women earned the right to vote.
    - Ⓒ Some colleges opened their doors to women.
    - Ⓓ A woman was elected mayor of a town.

Lesson Objective (4:3)

15. For what is Susan B. Anthony most famous?
    - Ⓐ working as a spy during World War I
    - Ⓑ climbing mountains all over the world
    - Ⓒ becoming the first woman mayor in the United States
    - ● working for women's suffrage

Part 2: Skills Test
Directions: Use complete sentences to answer questions 1–5. Use a separate sheet of paper if you need more space.

1. Complete the chart below. Compare and contrast Booker T. Washington and W. E. B. Du Bois. **Compare and Contrast**

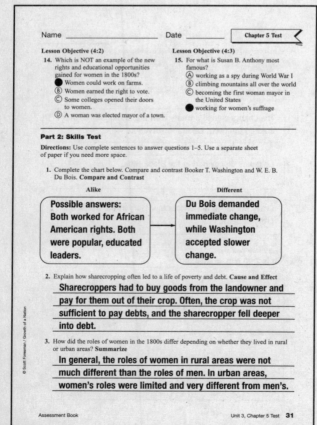

Alike	Different
Possible answers: Both worked for African American rights. Both were popular, educated leaders.	Du Bois demanded immediate change, while Washington accepted slower change.

2. Explain how sharecropping often led to a life of poverty and debt. **Cause and Effect**

   Sharecroppers had to buy goods from the landowner and pay for them out of their crop. Often, the crop was not sufficient to pay debts, and the sharecropper fell deeper into debt.

3. How did the roles of women in the 1800s differ depending on whether they lived in rural or urban areas? **Summarize**

   In general, the roles of women in rural areas were not much different than the roles of men. In urban areas, women's roles were limited and very different from men's.

---

4. What can you conclude from the fact that many African Americans in the South did not accept the idea of "separate but equal"? **Draw Conclusions**

   Possible answer: Separate facilities were not considered equal by African Americans.

5. Look at the graph below. In which year did the urban population first become greater than the rural population? **Read a Line Graph**

   Urban population surpassed rural population sometime between 1910 and 1940.

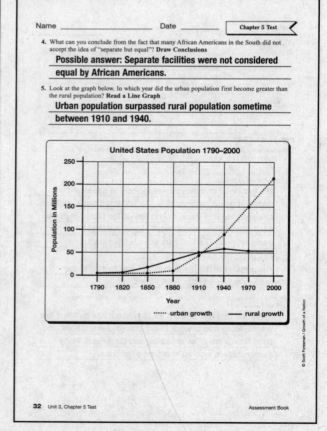

United States Population 1790–2000

---

84 Answer Key

Assessment Book

Chapter 6 Test
Part 1: Content Test
Directions: Fill in the circle next to the correct answer.

Lesson Objective (1:1)
1. Which of the following did NOT come under United States control in the late 1800s?
   - (A) Puerto Rico
   - (B) Alaska
   - ● Cuba
   - (D) Hawaii

Lesson Objective (1:2)
2. What eventually drew settlers to areas of Alaska?
   - (A) large cities
   - (B) war
   - ● gold
   - (D) farmland

Lesson Objective (1:3)
3. Yellow journalism helped contribute to the start of the Spanish-American War by
   - ● inflaming public opinion in the United States against Spain.
   - (B) providing an accurate and thorough record of events in Cuba.
   - (C) uncovering the truth about what happened to the *Maine*.
   - (D) forcing the Spanish to negotiate.

Lesson Objective (1:4)
4. Which of the following was NOT a result of the Spanish-American War?
   - ● The United States was no longer viewed as a powerful nation.
   - (B) Theodore Roosevelt became a national hero.
   - (C) The United States gained control of Puerto Rico, the Philippines, and Guam.
   - (D) The United States proved that it was a powerful nation.

Lesson Objective (2:1)
5. Which of the following is NOT a reform that occurred during the Roosevelt presidency?
   - (A) the Meat Inspection Act
   - ● the end of income tax
   - (C) the Pure Food and Drug Act
   - (D) improvement of education for children

Lesson Objective (2:1)
6. Why was Roosevelt convinced that he must break up trusts?
   - (A) Trusts weren't making enough money.
   - (B) He was afraid of Progressives.
   - (C) He felt leaders of trusts would eventually drive him from office.
   - ● Trusts were driving out competition and charging unfair prices.

Lesson Objective (2:2)
7. Who is the muckraker who wrote a series of articles about the dangers of trusts?
   - (A) John Muir
   - (B) Upton Sinclair
   - ● Ida Tarbell
   - (D) Theodore Roosevelt

Lesson Objective (2:2)
8. With what is Progressive Upton Sinclair credited?
   - ● writing a novel called *The Jungle* that told about conditions in the meatpacking plants of Chicago
   - (B) signing various reform acts and speaking out against trusts
   - (C) writing a series of articles about coal mining
   - (D) creating Blue Laws

Lesson Objective (2:3)
9. Which of the following is NOT one of the ways in which the Progressive Movement changed workplaces?
   - (A) Coal mines were inspected.
   - (B) Building codes made factories safer.
   - (C) Young children were kept from working in factories.
   - ● Children could work in factories as long as they attended school.

Lesson Objective (2:4)
10. Which of the following was NOT one of the accomplishments of Progressives?
    - (A) income tax
    - ● larger companies
    - (C) Blue Laws
    - (D) building codes

Lesson Objective (3:1)
11. Which of the following was NOT one of the factors that helped set the stage for the outbreak of World War I?
    - (A) growing nationalism in Europe
    - (B) competition between the nations of Europe
    - (C) alliances among different nations of Europe
    - ● isolationism among the nations of Europe

Lesson Objective (3:1)
12. During World War I, what did the countries of Great Britain, France, Russia, Serbia, and Belgium become known as?
    - (A) the Central Alliance
    - ● the Allied Powers
    - (C) the Central Powers
    - (D) the European Alliance

Lesson Objective (3:2)
13. Which is NOT one of the reasons why the United States decided to break its policy of isolationism and enter World War I?
    - (A) A German submarine sank the British steamship *Lusitania* and killed more than 100 U.S. citizens.
    - (B) Germany promised to help Mexico get back lands it had lost to the United States.
    - ● Immigrants in the United States were born in some of the countries that were fighting the war.
    - (D) German submarines sank three American-owned trade ships.

Lesson Objective (3:3)
14. What is one example of the way in which new technologies in World War I changed the way battles were fought?
    - (A) Soldiers dug trenches.
    - (B) Soldiers traveled by sea.
    - (C) Guns were used regularly in battle.
    - ● Airplanes became a weapon of war.

Lesson Objective (3:4)
15. Which is NOT a true statement about the impact of World War I in the United States?
    - (A) Some women went to work in factories to take over jobs men had done.
    - ● Most Americans argued against the war and refused to support the war effort in any way.
    - (C) The government set up a Food Administration to encourage people to eat less and send food to soldiers.
    - (D) People started growing food in "war gardens" to send to soldiers fighting overseas.

Part 2: Skills Test
Directions: Use complete sentences to answer questions 1–5. Use a separate sheet of paper if you need more space.

1. What was the effect of the Spanish-American War on the United States and its place in the world? **Cause and Effect**

   The United States emerged from the Spanish-American War as a major world power.

2. Summarize the actions of the United States throughout World War I. **Summarize**

   The United States originally chose to avoid involvement in World War I. German attacks on shipping and attempts to draw Mexico into the conflict finally led the United States to join the war. Once involved in the fighting, the United States helped turn the tide and bring victory to the Allies.

3. Complete the chart below. Compare and contrast the U.S. acquisition of Hawaii and Alaska. **Compare and Contrast**

Alike	Different
Possible answers: Alike: Both were lands far from the United States. Many people in the United States wanted to control them because both held promise of valuable resources.	**Alaska's resources were largely unknown, while Hawaii was already being used by Americans. Hawaii somewhat resisted the United States takeover, whereas Alaska was acquired through agreement with its owner.**

4. Suppose you are living in the United States during the Theodore Roosevelt era. You don't know much about the activities of the Progressives and want to gather background information about them. Which of the following sources is probably most credible for this purpose? For what might the other sources be useful? Explain your reasoning on the lines that follow. **Credibility of a Source**

   A piece by the owner of a large company that must now follow new rules.

   A news article by a reporter who is looking at only facts.

   A letter by a factory worker whose work conditions have improved as a result of the Progressives.

   The news article that presents only the facts would probably be the best source of general information about the Progressives. The other pieces would be useful in presenting different views on the activities of the Progressives, but they probably wouldn't present the facts as clearly. The personal experiences of each writer would affect the information in each piece.

5. What is a political cartoon? Write your answer on the lines provided. Then, in the space below, draw a political cartoon that tries to get people thinking about the problems of industrial society in the early 1900s. Think about what details you might include in your cartoon in order to make your point. **Interpret Political Cartoons**

   Students should understand that a political cartoon is a drawing that shows people or events in the news in a way that often makes people smile or laugh.

   Students' drawings will vary.

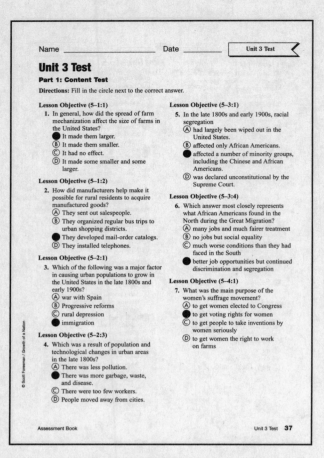
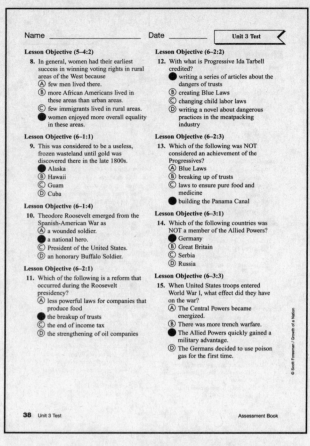
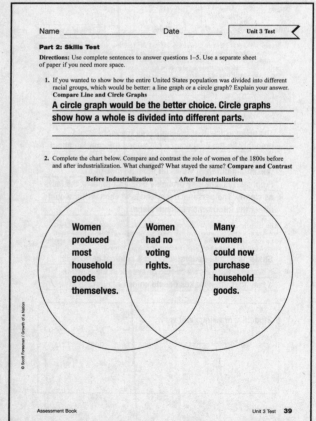
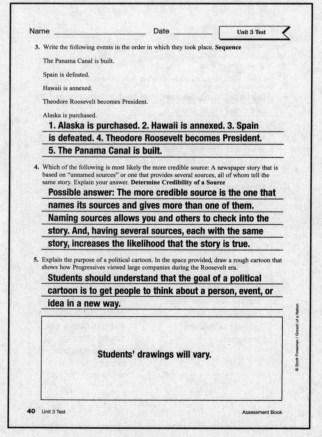

Chapter 7 Test

Part 1: Content Test

Directions: Fill in the circle next to the correct answer.

Lesson Objective (1:1)

1. What allowed Henry Ford's Model Ts to be sold for less than half the cost of other cars?
   - Ⓐ the use of cheaper materials
   - ● the use of an assembly line
   - Ⓒ not following safety standards
   - Ⓓ the fact that no two cars were exactly alike

Lesson Objective (1:2)

2. Which of the following is NOT a way in which the automobile changed life in the United States?
   - ● Farmers had to carry their crops to market.
   - Ⓑ Roads were improved.
   - Ⓒ It created many new jobs.
   - Ⓓ People moved farther from their jobs.

Lesson Objective (1:3)

3. Why were romantic dramas nicknamed "soap operas"?
   - Ⓐ Most people watched them at the laundromat.
   - Ⓑ They encouraged people to go to the opera.
   - Ⓒ They were often paid for by opera companies.
   - ● They were often paid for by soap companies.

Lesson Objective (2:1)

4. Which of the following describes a reason why Prohibition failed?
   - ● Police had little success in stopping bootleggers.
   - Ⓑ Many bootleggers moved their businesses to Canada.
   - Ⓒ Many people moved to Europe, where they could still buy alcohol.
   - Ⓓ Many people spent their money on their families instead of on alcohol.

Lesson Objective (2:2)

5. Which musician recorded "St. Louis Blues" with Bessie Smith?
   - Ⓐ Duke Ellington
   - ● Louis Armstrong
   - Ⓒ George Gershwin
   - Ⓓ Aaron Copland

Lesson Objective (2:2)

6. Which Harlem Renaissance figure created several series of paintings that showed African American life and history?
   - ● Jacob Lawrence
   - Ⓑ Langston Hughes
   - Ⓒ Zora Neale Hurston
   - Ⓓ James Weldon Johnson

Lesson Objective (2:3)

7. How did mass media help make athletes popular in the 1920s?
   - Ⓐ Most movies were about sports.
   - Ⓑ Many newspaper articles were paid for by sports teams.
   - Ⓒ Many athletes starred in radio dramas.
   - ● Radio made it possible for fans to listen to sports games.

Lesson Objective (2:4)

8. How did working life change for women in the 1920s?
   - Ⓐ A greater percentage of women joined the workforce.
   - Ⓑ Many women moved from farming to manufacturing.
   - ● Many women moved from factory work to office jobs.
   - Ⓓ Many women earned the same wages as men.

Lesson Objective (3:1)

9. Which of the following describes the economy in the 1920s?
   - Ⓐ The mining industry grew as coal replaced oil for fuel.
   - Ⓑ The lumber industry grew as builders began using wood instead of concrete.
   - ● Crop prices fell and many farmers had difficulty paying off debts.
   - Ⓓ Factory workers were unable to produce enough goods.

Lesson Objective (3:2)

10. Which of the following describes what happened during the stock market crash of 1929?
    - ● Stock prices fell and many investors sold their stocks.
    - Ⓑ Stock prices rose and many investors sold their stocks.
    - Ⓒ Stock prices fell and many investors purchased stocks.
    - Ⓓ Stock prices rose and many investors purchased stocks.

Lesson Objective (3:3)

11. Which of the following was NOT a cause of the Great Depression?
    - Ⓐ The stock market crashed.
    - Ⓑ High tariffs were placed on imported and exported goods.
    - Ⓒ Many people borrowed money from banks, which they could not pay back.
    - ● There was a sharp increase in the price of manufactured goods.

Lesson Objective (3:4)

12. Which of the following describes a way in which the Great Depression affected the lives of many Americans?
    - Ⓐ Many people moved from shantytowns to suburbs.
    - ● Many children quit school to help their families earn money.
    - Ⓒ More people got married immediately after high school or college.
    - Ⓓ Farmers were hurt by the effects of tariffs and rising crop prices.

Lesson Objective (4:1)

13. Which New Deal program provided monthly payments to the elderly, disabled, and unemployed?
    - Ⓐ Farm Security Administration
    - ● Social Security
    - Ⓒ Securities and Exchange Commission
    - Ⓓ Works Progress Administration

Lesson Objective (4:2)

14. What was an effect of the Dust Bowl?
    - Ⓐ Many factories laid off workers.
    - Ⓑ Many families left California and headed east.
    - ● Many people became migrant workers.
    - Ⓓ Many farmers moved to the Great Plains.

Lesson Objective (4:3)

15. Which new form of entertainment in the 1930s included characters such as Superman and Batman?
    - Ⓐ the movie
    - Ⓑ the World's Fair
    - Ⓒ the board game
    - ● the comic book

Part 2: Skills Test

Directions: Use complete sentences to answer questions 1–5. Use a separate sheet of paper if you need more space.

1. Complete the chart below. Use the details to draw a conclusion about the effects of mass media in the United States. **Draw Conclusions**

Detail: People throughout the country bought the same products that were advertised on the radio.	Detail: The same songs, shows, and movies became popular across the entire nation.	Detail: Many people copied the hairstyles and clothing of their favorite movie stars.

Conclusion:

Mass media encouraged a common American culture.

2. What were some effects of the Eighteenth Amendment? **Cause and Effect**

Levels of alcohol abuse declined in some areas. However, many people ignored the law. Bootleggers took over the alcohol business and sometimes sold alcohol that was dangerous. Violent clashes sometimes occurred among bootleggers. The amendment was repealed in 1933.

3. Read the passage. Write one fact and one opinion in the space provided. **Fact and Opinion**

> F. Scott Fitzgerald was a talented writer. His novels include *This Side of Paradise*, *The Great Gatsby*, and *Tender Is the Night*. *The Great Gatsby* is by far his best work. It tells a story about New York life during the Roaring Twenties.

Fact:

Possible answer: His novels include *This Side of Paradise*, *The Great Gatsby*, and *Tender Is the Night*.

Opinion:

Possible answer: *The Great Gatsby* is by far his best work.

4. How did Franklin D. Roosevelt try to help the country through the Great Depression? **Summarize**

Roosevelt believed that the government needed to play a greater role in helping the country through the depression. His New Deal programs focused on relief, recovery, and reform. Relief programs provided assistance to those in need. Recovery efforts were aimed at improving the economy. Reform laws were designed to correct weaknesses that had led to the depression.

5. What caused the Dust Bowl? **Cause and Effect**

Severe drought and high winds throughout the Great Plains caused the Dust Bowl.

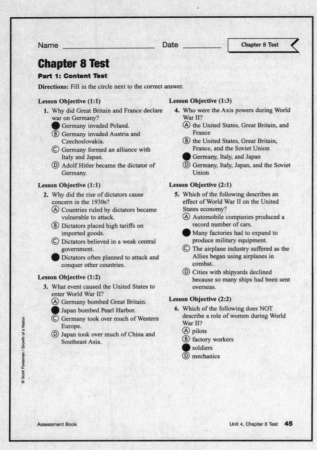

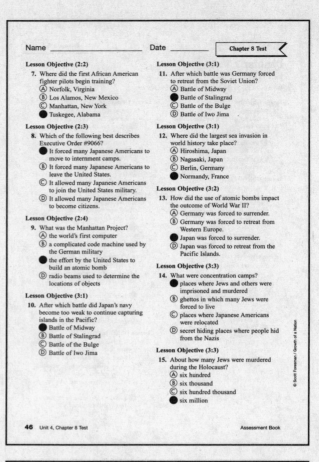

Chapter 8 Test

Part 1: Content Test

Directions: Fill in the circle next to the correct answer.

Lesson Objective (1:1)

1. Why did Great Britain and France declare war on Germany?
   - ● Germany invaded Poland.
   - Ⓑ Germany invaded Austria and Czechoslovakia.
   - Ⓒ Germany formed an alliance with Italy and Japan.
   - Ⓓ Adolf Hitler became the dictator of Germany.

Lesson Objective (1:1)

2. Why did the rise of dictators cause concern in the 1930s?
   - Ⓐ Countries ruled by dictators became vulnerable to attack.
   - Ⓑ Dictators placed high tariffs on imported goods.
   - Ⓒ Dictators believed in a weak central government.
   - ● Dictators often planned to attack and conquer other countries.

Lesson Objective (1:2)

3. What event caused the United States to enter World War II?
   - Ⓐ Germany bombed Great Britain.
   - ● Japan bombed Pearl Harbor.
   - Ⓒ Germany took over much of Western Europe.
   - Ⓓ Japan took over much of China and Southeast Asia.

Lesson Objective (1:3)

4. Who were the Axis powers during World War II?
   - Ⓐ the United States, Great Britain, and France
   - Ⓑ the United States, Great Britain, France, and the Soviet Union
   - ● Germany, Italy, and Japan
   - Ⓓ Germany, Italy, Japan, and the Soviet Union

Lesson Objective (2:1)

5. Which of the following describes an effect of World War II on the United States economy?
   - Ⓐ Automobile companies produced a record number of cars.
   - ● Many factories had to expand to produce military equipment.
   - Ⓒ The airplane industry suffered as the Allies began using airplanes in combat.
   - Ⓓ Cities with shipyards declined because so many ships had been sent overseas.

Lesson Objective (2:2)

6. Which of the following does NOT describe a role of women during World War II?
   - Ⓐ pilots
   - Ⓑ factory workers
   - ● soldiers
   - Ⓓ mechanics

Lesson Objective (2:2)

7. Where did the first African American fighter pilots begin training?
   - Ⓐ Norfolk, Virginia
   - Ⓑ Los Alamos, New Mexico
   - Ⓒ Manhattan, New York
   - ● Tuskegee, Alabama

Lesson Objective (2:3)

8. Which of the following best describes Executive Order #9066?
   - ● It forced many Japanese Americans to move to internment camps.
   - Ⓑ It forced many Japanese Americans to leave the United States.
   - Ⓒ It allowed many Japanese Americans to join the United States military.
   - Ⓓ It allowed many Japanese Americans to become citizens.

Lesson Objective (2:4)

9. What was the Manhattan Project?
   - Ⓐ the world's first computer
   - Ⓑ a complicated code machine used by the German military
   - ● the effort by the United States to build an atomic bomb
   - Ⓓ radio beams used to determine the locations of objects

Lesson Objective (3:1)

10. After which battle did Japan's navy become too weak to continue capturing islands in the Pacific?
    - ● Battle of Midway
    - Ⓑ Battle of Stalingrad
    - Ⓒ Battle of the Bulge
    - Ⓓ Battle of Iwo Jima

Lesson Objective (3:1)

11. After which battle was Germany forced to retreat from the Soviet Union?
    - Ⓐ Battle of Midway
    - ● Battle of Stalingrad
    - Ⓒ Battle of the Bulge
    - Ⓓ Battle of Iwo Jima

Lesson Objective (3:1)

12. Where did the largest sea invasion in world history take place?
    - Ⓐ Hiroshima, Japan
    - Ⓑ Nagasaki, Japan
    - Ⓒ Berlin, Germany
    - ● Normandy, France

Lesson Objective (3:2)

13. How did the use of atomic bombs impact the outcome of World War II?
    - Ⓐ Germany was forced to surrender.
    - Ⓑ Germany was forced to retreat from Western Europe.
    - ● Japan was forced to surrender.
    - Ⓓ Japan was forced to retreat from the Pacific Islands.

Lesson Objective (3:3)

14. What were concentration camps?
    - ● places where Jews and others were imprisoned and murdered
    - Ⓑ ghettos in which many Jews were forced to live
    - Ⓒ places where Japanese Americans were relocated
    - Ⓓ secret hiding places where people hid from the Nazis

Lesson Objective (3:3)

15. About how many Jews were murdered during the Holocaust?
    - Ⓐ six hundred
    - Ⓑ six thousand
    - Ⓒ six hundred thousand
    - ● six million

Part 2: Skills Test

Directions: Use complete sentences to answer questions 1–5. Use a separate sheet of paper if you need more space.

1. How did World War II change life for many women and African Americans? **Summarize**

   World War II created new opportunities for many women and African Americans. Women served in the military, took factory jobs, and played professional baseball. African Americans took factory jobs and earned more money than they ever had before. They also served in the military, and some became fighter pilots.

2. Complete the chart below. Use the details to draw a conclusion about Americans on the home front during World War II. **Draw Conclusions**

Detail: Many children organized "scrap drives."	Detail: Millions of Americans planted Victory Gardens.	Detail: Families rationed goods.

   Conclusion:
   During World War II, Americans on the home front worked hard to help the war effort.

3. Why did President Truman decide to use the atomic bomb? **Main Idea and Details**

   He hoped that it would make an invasion unnecessary and save American lives. He also hoped that it would force Japan to surrender.

4. Write the following events in the order in which they happened. **Sequence**

   Allied forces led an invasion in Normandy, France.

   George S. Patton led the Allies to victory at the Battle of the Bulge.

   The Allies defeated Axis forces in North Africa and Italy.

   The Allies defeated Axis forces in North Africa and Italy.
   Allied forces led an invasion in Normandy, France.
   George S. Patton led the Allies to victory at the Battle of the Bulge.

5. Look at the map below. Describe the location of the equator. Which two World War II battles took place closest to the equator? **Understand Key Lines of Latitude and Longitude**

   The equator is found at the center of Earth, at latitude 0°. The battles at Tarawa and Borneo were closest to the equator.

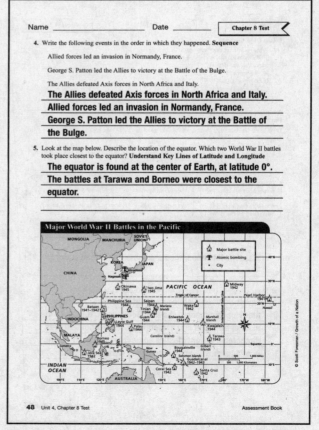

© Scott Foresman / Growth of a Nation

Unit 4 Test

Part 1: Content Test

Directions: Fill in the circle next to the correct answer.

Lesson Objective (7–1:1)

1. How did the assembly line change American industry?
   - Ⓐ It increased the cost of manufactured products.
   - ● It allowed companies to manufacture large numbers of identical products.
   - Ⓒ It caused an increase in unemployment.
   - Ⓓ It forced many factory workers to take a cut in pay.

Lesson Objective (7–1:2)

2. How did the automobile change life in the United States?
   - Ⓐ Many farmers were unable to get their crops to market.
   - Ⓑ Many people were able to move closer to their jobs.
   - ● The manufacture of automobiles helped create many new jobs.
   - Ⓓ The increase in car ownership led to a decline in tourism.

Lesson Objective (7–2:1)

3. Which event did NOT lead to the passage of the Eighteenth Amendment?
   - Ⓐ Many were concerned that people abused alcohol.
   - Ⓑ Many were concerned that people spent money on alcohol instead of on their families.
   - Ⓒ Progressive reformers helped pass Blue Laws.
   - ● Bootleggers competed for business with the speakeasies.

Lesson Objective (7–2:2)

4. Which of the following describes the achievements of Zora Neale Hurston?
   - Ⓐ created several series of paintings that showed African American life and history
   - ● wrote about the experiences of African Americans
   - Ⓒ made several recordings with Louis Armstrong
   - Ⓓ wrote concert music such as "Rhapsody in Blue"

Lesson Objective (7–3:2)

5. During the stock market crash of 1929
   - Ⓐ many investors panicked and purchased stocks.
   - ● many investors panicked and sold their stocks.
   - Ⓒ the market froze because people were afraid to buy or sell stocks.
   - Ⓓ stock prices rose and investors could no longer afford them.

Lesson Objective (7–3:3)

6. Which of the following was a cause of the Great Depression?
   - ● Many investors had purchased stocks on credit.
   - Ⓑ Congress reduced tariffs on foreign goods.
   - Ⓒ Many farmers were unable to produce enough crops.
   - Ⓓ Many factories faced a shortage of workers.

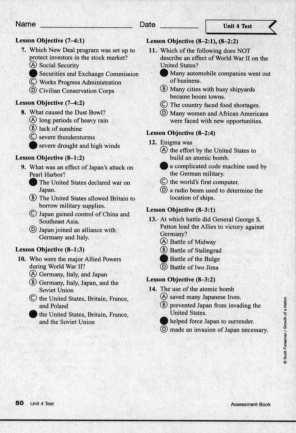

Lesson Objective (7–4:1)

7. Which New Deal program was set up to protect investors in the stock market?
   - Ⓐ Social Security
   - ● Securities and Exchange Commission
   - Ⓒ Works Progress Administration
   - Ⓓ Civilian Conservation Corps

Lesson Objective (7–4:2)

8. What caused the Dust Bowl?
   - Ⓐ long periods of heavy rain
   - Ⓑ lack of sunshine
   - Ⓒ severe thunderstorms
   - ● severe drought and high winds

Lesson Objective (8–1:2)

9. What was an effect of Japan's attack on Pearl Harbor?
   - ● The United States declared war on Japan.
   - Ⓑ The United States allowed Britain to borrow military supplies.
   - Ⓒ Japan gained control of China and Southeast Asia.
   - Ⓓ Japan joined an alliance with Germany and Italy.

Lesson Objective (8–1:3)

10. Who were the major Allied Powers during World War II?
    - Ⓐ Germany, Italy, and Japan
    - Ⓑ Germany, Italy, Japan, and the Soviet Union
    - Ⓒ the United States, Britain, France, and Poland
    - ● the United States, Britain, France, and the Soviet Union

Lesson Objective (8–2:1), (8–2:2)

11. Which of the following does NOT describe an effect of World War II on the United States?
    - ● Many automobile companies went out of business.
    - Ⓑ Many cities with busy shipyards became boom towns.
    - Ⓒ The country faced food shortages.
    - Ⓓ Many women and African Americans were faced with new opportunities.

Lesson Objective (8–2:4)

12. Enigma was
    - Ⓐ the effort by the United States to build an atomic bomb.
    - ● a complicated code machine used by the German military.
    - Ⓒ the world's first computer.
    - Ⓓ a radio beam used to determine the location of ships.

Lesson Objective (8–3:1)

13. At which battle did General George S. Patton lead the Allies to victory against Germany?
    - Ⓐ Battle of Midway
    - Ⓑ Battle of Stalingrad
    - ● Battle of the Bulge
    - Ⓓ Battle of Iwo Jima

Lesson Objective (8–3:2)

14. The use of the atomic bomb
    - Ⓐ saved many Japanese lives.
    - Ⓑ prevented Japan from invading the United States.
    - ● helped force Japan to surrender.
    - Ⓓ made an invasion of Japan necessary.

Lesson Objective (8–3:3)

15. During the Holocaust
    - Ⓐ about one million Jews were murdered.
    - Ⓑ about two million Jews were murdered.
    - Ⓒ about four million Jews were murdered.
    - ● about six million Jews were murdered.

Part 2: Skills Test

Directions: Use complete sentences to answer questions 1–5. Use a separate sheet of paper if you need more space.

1. Read the passage. Write one fact and one opinion in the space provided. **Fact and Opinion**

> On November 2, 1920, the first professional radio station in the world began broadcasting. This was an exciting day. Listeners were able to hear results of the U.S. presidential election. Radio stations soon began broadcasting music, dramas, and even sports programs. The best radio program was the action-adventure *Captain Midnight.*

Fact:
Possible answer: On November 2, 1920, the first professional radio station in the world began broadcasting.

Opinion:
Possible answer: This was an exciting day.

2. What is the purpose of using lines of latitude and longitude? What is the latitude of the equator? **Understand Key Lines of Latitude and Longitude**
These lines help people to locate places on maps accurately. The equator is at latitude 0°.

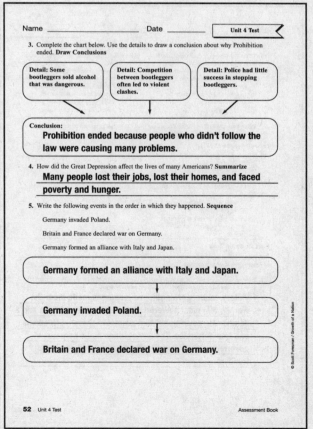

3. Complete the chart below. Use the details to draw a conclusion about why Prohibition ended. **Draw Conclusions**

Detail: Some bootleggers sold alcohol that was dangerous.

Detail: Competition between bootleggers often led to violent clashes.

Detail: Police had little success in stopping bootleggers.

Conclusion:
Prohibition ended because people who didn't follow the law were causing many problems.

4. How did the Great Depression affect the lives of many Americans? **Summarize**
Many people lost their jobs, lost their homes, and faced poverty and hunger.

5. Write the following events in the order in which they happened. **Sequence**

Germany invaded Poland.

Britain and France declared war on Germany.

Germany formed an alliance with Italy and Japan.

Germany formed an alliance with Italy and Japan.
↓
Germany invaded Poland.
↓
Britain and France declared war on Germany.

Chapter 9 Test

Part 1: Content Test

Directions: Fill in the circle next to the correct answer.

Lesson Objective (1:1)

1. Which of the following does NOT describe Europe after World War II?
   - ● Germany emerged as one of the world's most powerful nations.
   - Ⓑ Industries, farms, and homes were in ruins.
   - Ⓒ Many people were without food, clothing, and shelter.
   - Ⓓ Much of Eastern Europe fell to Soviet control.

Lesson Objective (1:1)

2. What was a main goal of the Marshall Plan?
   - Ⓐ to encourage the spread of communism in Europe
   - ● to help Europe recover from the war
   - Ⓒ to help Japan recover from the war
   - Ⓓ to help Japan set up a democratic government

Lesson Objective (1:2)

3. Which of the following describes the United States after World War II?
   - Ⓐ Much of the United States was in ruins.
   - Ⓑ The United States emerged from the war as one of the world's weakest nations.
   - Ⓒ The United States gained control of Japan and Eastern Europe.
   - ● The United States emerged from the war as a superpower.

Lesson Objective (1:3)

4. What was a main purpose in forming the United Nations?
   - Ⓐ to create a plan for rebuilding Europe and Japan
   - ● to create an organization that would promote global cooperation
   - Ⓒ to create an iron curtain between communist and noncommunist countries
   - Ⓓ to create a military alliance against the Soviet Union

Lesson Objective (1:4)

5. What was the Cold War?
   - ● a long, bitter struggle between the United States and the Soviet Union
   - Ⓑ an armed conflict between the United States and the Soviet Union
   - Ⓒ a period in which many Asian and European nations established communist governments
   - Ⓓ a period in which many Free World nations became Third World nations

Lesson Objective (1:4)

6. Which of the following describes a difference in ideology between Soviets and Americans?
   - Ⓐ Soviets believed in free enterprise and Americans believed in democracy.
   - Ⓑ Soviets believed in communism and Americans believed in little personal freedom.
   - ● Soviets believed in communism and Americans believed in democracy.
   - Ⓓ Soviets wanted to work for peace and Americans wanted an iron curtain.

Lesson Objective (2:1)

7. Which of the following did NOT contribute to the growth of the American economy following World War II?
   - Ⓐ Many families wanted to buy new homes.
   - ● The number of returning veterans resulted in a shortage of jobs.
   - Ⓒ Industries could focus on producing consumer goods instead of war materials.
   - Ⓓ Rationing had ended.

Lesson Objective (2:2)

8. Which of the following is NOT a way in which Americans changed the way they lived in the 1950s?
   - Ⓐ Many placed a greater emphasis on education.
   - Ⓑ Many used credit cards to charge goods and services.
   - ● Many moved from suburbs to cities.
   - Ⓓ Many enjoyed more leisure time.

Lesson Objective (2:3)

9. Which statement describes the automotive industry in the 1950s?
   - Ⓐ The automotive industry declined because public transportation became more widely available.
   - Ⓑ The automotive industry declined as focus shifted from developing peacetime technologies to war technologies.
   - Ⓒ Many engineers left the automotive industry to design fighter planes.
   - ● New technologies such as automatic transmission, radial tires, and power steering were introduced.

Lesson Objective (2:4)

10. Which of the following is NOT a way in which new technologies changed life for Americans in the 1950s?
    - ● Most households had Internet access.
    - Ⓑ Most households had televisions.
    - Ⓒ Many households had air conditioning systems.
    - Ⓓ Many people began to use commercial airlines.

Lesson Objective (3:1)

11. Which event led to the Korean War?
    - Ⓐ South Koreans invaded communist North Korea.
    - ● Communist North Koreans invaded South Korea.
    - Ⓒ The United States and its allies invaded communist South Korea.
    - Ⓓ Communist Chinese forces invaded South Korea.

Lesson Objective (3:1)

12. Which of the following occurred at the end of the Korean War?
    - Ⓐ Korea was united under a democratic government.
    - Ⓑ Korea was united under a communist government.
    - ● United States troops helped guard the border zone between North Korea and South Korea.
    - Ⓓ Chinese troops helped guard the border zone between North Korea and South Korea.

Lesson Objective (3:1)

13. What was the purpose of the Southeast Asia Treaty Organization?
    - Ⓐ to ease Cold War tensions between the United States and the Soviet Union
    - Ⓑ to form an alliance against the United States
    - Ⓒ to create a blockade against western nations
    - ● to protect Southeast Asian countries against the spread of communism

Lesson Objective (3:2)

14. Which of the following did NOT occur during the Red Scare?
    - Ⓐ Many communists were arrested.
    - Ⓑ Many innocent people were investigated and sometimes bullied.
    - ● Investigators learned that Senator Joseph McCarthy was a communist spy.
    - Ⓓ People who refused to cooperate with investigations often lost their jobs.

Lesson Objective (3:3)

15. Which event led to the Cuban Missile Crisis?
    - ● Soviets were setting up nuclear missiles in Cuba.
    - Ⓑ Cubans were setting up nuclear missiles in the Soviet Union.
    - Ⓒ The United States formed an alliance with Cuba against the Soviet Union.
    - Ⓓ The Soviet Union and the United States agreed to stop building nuclear weapons.

Part 2: Skills Test

Directions: Use complete sentences to answer questions 1–5. Use a separate sheet of paper if you need more space.

1. In what ways were the United States and the Soviet Union similar after World War II? In what ways were they different? **Compare and Contrast**

   Victory, military strength, and resources made them the world's two most powerful nations. The United States had a democratic government that promoted personal freedoms and free enterprise. The Soviet Union had a communist government that allowed little personal and economic freedom.

---

2. Complete the cause and effect chart below. Identify a cause of the Berlin Airlift.
   Cause and Effect

   > **Cause:**
   > **The Soviets blockaded western Berlin.**

   ↓

   > **Effect: The Americans and British flew food and fuel into West Berlin.**

3. Describe the similarities and differences between primary and secondary sources.
   Compare Primary and Secondary Sources

   Both are valuable sources of information. A primary source is an eyewitness account that can offer emotion and vivid descriptions. A secondary source is a secondhand account that often uses broad descriptions and draws on multiple sources of information.

4. How did the G.I. Bill of Rights help men and women who had served in the military?
   Main Idea and Details

   The law helped veterans succeed in civilian society by offering benefits such as education and training, guaranteed loans, unemployment pay, and job-finding assistance.

5. Why do you think American leaders felt it was important to stay ahead of the Soviet Union in the arms race? **Draw Conclusions**

   Possible answer: Many felt that if the United States had more powerful weapons than the Soviets, then the Soviets would be less likely to attack.

Chapter 10 Test

Part 1: Content Test

Directions: Fill in the circle next to the correct answer.

Lesson Objective (1:1)

1. Which of the following was a cause of the civil rights movement?
   ● African Americans were often denied equal rights.
   Ⓑ President Roosevelt ordered an end to discrimination in all defense industries.
   Ⓒ Many were upset with the Supreme Court's decision in *Brown* v. *Board of Education*.
   Ⓓ Congress passed the Voting Rights Act of 1964.

Lesson Objective (1:2)

2. Which of the following is NOT a way in which segregation affected American society?
   Ⓐ Blacks and whites had to attend separate schools.
   Ⓑ Blacks and whites were socially isolated.
   Ⓒ Blacks and whites had to use separate public facilities.
   ● Blacks and whites had to ride different public buses.

Lesson Objective (1:3)

3. Which of the following events occurred last?
   Ⓐ President Truman ordered an end to segregation of the United States military.
   ● Martin Luther King, Jr., helped plan a massive march in Washington, D.C.
   Ⓒ Rosa Parks refused to give up her seat on a Montgomery bus.
   Ⓓ Segregation of public schools was declared illegal.

Lesson Objective (1:4)

4. Which of the following describes the Civil Rights Act of 1964?
   Ⓐ Supreme Court ruling that segregation of public buses was illegal
   Ⓑ Supreme Court ruling that protected the rights of all Americans to vote
   ● law passed by Congress that banned segregation in all public places in the United States
   Ⓓ law passed by Congress that banned the use of passive resistance

Lesson Objective (2:1)

5. What was the space race?
   Ⓐ race between the United States and the Soviet Union to build weapons
   Ⓑ race between the United States and China to gain control of Asian territory
   ● race between the United States and the Soviet Union to explore outer space
   Ⓓ race between the United States and China to explore outer space

Lesson Objective (2:2)

6. Why did the United States send soldiers to Vietnam?
   ● North Vietnamese were fighting to unite Vietnam under a communist government.
   Ⓑ South Vietnamese were fighting to unite Vietnam under a communist government.
   Ⓒ The Soviet Union had sent forces into South Vietnam.
   Ⓓ China had gained control of North Vietnam and threatened to invade South Vietnam.

Lesson Objective (2:3)

7. Which of the following did NOT occur after the last American troops left Vietnam?
   Ⓐ The North Vietnamese and the South Vietnamese continued fighting.
   Ⓑ South Vietnam surrendered to North Vietnam.
   ● Henry Kissinger met with North Vietnamese and Viet Cong leaders in Paris.
   Ⓓ Vietnam was united under a communist government.

Lesson Objective (2:4)

8. Which statement best describes the doves' position toward the Vietnam Conflict?
   ● They believed it was a civil war that should be settled by the Vietnamese people.
   Ⓑ They believed it was a civil war that should be settled by China and the Soviet Union.
   Ⓒ They believed it was necessary to stop the spread of communism.
   Ⓓ They believed the United States should station troops along the Chinese border.

Lesson Objective (3:1)

9. Which statement best describes the role of women in the mid-1900s?
   Ⓐ Women had the same opportunities as men.
   Ⓑ The number of women in the workplace continued to decrease.
   Ⓒ Women often earned higher wages than men.
   ● Women were not allowed to participate in certain sports.

Lesson Objective (3:2)

10. Which of the following is NOT an achievement of the Women's Rights Movement of the mid-1900s?
    Ⓐ The National Organization for Women was formed.
    Ⓑ Congress passed the Title 9 law.
    ● The Equal Rights Amendment was ratified.
    Ⓓ More job opportunities became available for women.

Lesson Objective (3:3)

11. What was the purpose of the National Farm Workers Association?
    Ⓐ to gain rights for Americans with disabilities
    ● to gain rights for migrant workers
    Ⓒ to gain rights for American Indians
    Ⓓ to gain rights for Japanese Americans

Lesson Objective (3:4)

12. Which of the following is NOT a way in which Americans worked to improve the environment in the late 1900s?
    Ⓐ The Environmental Protection Agency was formed.
    ● Congress passed mandatory recycling laws.
    Ⓒ The first Earth Day was celebrated.
    Ⓓ Rachel Carson wrote *Silent Spring*.

Lesson Objective (4:1)

13. Which statement does NOT describe President Nixon's trip to China?
    Ⓐ It was the first time an American President visited China.
    Ⓑ It was an important step toward friendlier relations with China.
    ● Nixon signed an arms control agreement with Chinese leaders.
    Ⓓ Nixon met with communist leader Mao Zedong.

Lesson Objective (4:2)

14. Why did President Carter invite the leaders of Egypt and Israel to the United States?
    Ⓐ to form a military alliance with the two nations
    Ⓑ to try to improve trade relations with the two nations
    Ⓒ to help the two nations overthrow their communist governments
    ● to try to help bring peace between the two nations

Lesson Objective (4:3)

15. Which of the following did NOT lead to the collapse of communism in the 1990s?
    ● Cold War tensions increased.
    Ⓑ The Soviet economy was weakened by the high cost of the arms race.
    Ⓒ Mikhail Gorbachev came to power.
    Ⓓ People in Eastern Europe gained more freedom.

Part 2: Skills Test

Directions: Use complete sentences to answer questions 1–5. Use a separate sheet of paper if you need more space.

1. Identify three ways in which African Americans used passive resistance to gain civil rights. **Main Idea and Details**
   They organized sit-ins, freedom rides, and marches.

2. Explain how the Vietnam Conflict divided many Americans. **Summarize**
   Many disagreed over whether the United States should continue fighting. Doves believed the conflict was a civil war that should be settled by the Vietnamese people. Hawks believed that the war was necessary to stop the spread of communism.

3. Write the following events in the order in which they happened. **Sequence**
   The Berlin Wall was destroyed.
   The United States and the Soviet Union agreed to destroy some of their nuclear weapons.
   The Soviet Union broke up into 15 independent republics.
   Communist governments fell in several Eastern European nations.
   The United States and the Soviet Union agreed to destroy some of their nuclear weapons. Communist governments fell in several Eastern European nations. The Berlin Wall was destroyed. The Soviet Union broke up into 15 independent republics.

4. Complete the cause-and-effect chart below. Identify an effect of Iraq's invasion of Kuwait. **Cause and Effect**

   Cause: Saddam Hussein refused to withdraw his troops from Kuwait.

   ↓

   Effect: **The United States led an alliance to drive Iraqi forces from Kuwait.**

5. Study the maps below. Describe the differences between the two maps. **Understand Map Projections**
   The equal-area projection tries to correct the distortions of the Mercator projection by showing the longitude lines curving toward the poles. The Mercator projection shows longitude and latitude lines that are parallel to one another. Distances, shapes, and sizes are fairly accurate near the equator but become distorted toward the poles.

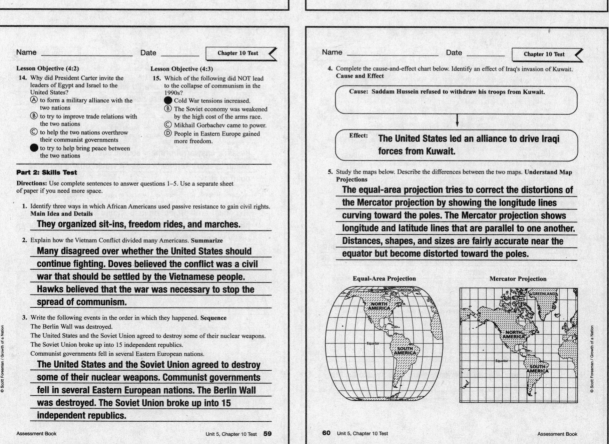

Equal-Area Projection

Mercator Projection

Unit 5 Test

Part 1: Content Test

Directions: Fill in the circle next to the correct answer.

Lesson Objective (9–1:1)

1. Which of the following describes Japan after World War II?
   - (A) Japan adopted a communist government.
   - ● Japan adopted a democratic government.
   - (C) Japan was divided into North Japan and South Japan.
   - (D) Japan emerged from the war as one of the world's most powerful nations.

Lesson Objective (9–1:2)

2. Which statement describes the role of the United States after World War II?
   - ● Victory, military strength, and resources made the United States a superpower.
   - (B) The United States demanded control over its bordering countries.
   - (C) The United States controlled much of Eastern and Central Europe.
   - (D) The United States stationed advisors in the Soviet Union to help with their recovery.

Lesson Objective (9–1:4)

3. Which of the following describes a cause of Cold War tensions?
   - (A) The Soviet Union believed in personal freedoms and the United States did not.
   - (B) The Soviet Union believed in free enterprise and the United States did not.
   - (C) The United States supported communism and the Soviet Union did not.
   - ● The United States supported freely elected governments and the Soviet Union did not.

Lesson Objective (9–2:1)

4. Which of the following contributed to the rapid growth of the American economy after World War II?
   - ● Many felt confident about the future and began spending more money.
   - (B) Industries that had produced consumer goods were able to focus on producing war materials.
   - (C) Many people moved from suburbs to cities.
   - (D) Many families rationed goods such as food and clothing.

Lesson Objective (9–2:4)

5. Which of the following is NOT a new technology that improved life for Americans in the 1950s?
   - (A) air conditioning
   - (B) better heating systems
   - (C) coast-to-coast direct dial telephone service
   - ● electric streetcar

Lesson Objective (9–3:1)

6. How did the Korean War relate to the Cold War?
   - (A) The Soviet Union joined South Korean forces to help stop the spread of democracy.
   - (B) The Soviet union joined North Korean forces to help stop the spread of communism.
   - ● The United States joined South Korean forces to help stop the spread of communism.
   - (D) The United States joined North Korean forces to help stop the spread of democracy.

Lesson Objective (9–3:2)

7. How did Cold War tensions affect Americans at home?
   - (A) All Americans were forced to take an oath of loyalty to the government.
   - (B) Americans were not allowed to travel outside of United States borders.
   - (C) Communist revolutions took place in several major cities.
   - ● Many feared that communist spies were working inside the government.

Lesson Objective (9–3:3)

8. How did President Kennedy respond to information that the Soviets were setting up nuclear missiles in Cuba?
   - ● He insisted that the Soviets remove their missiles.
   - (B) He signed a peace treaty with Fidel Castro.
   - (C) He declared that the United States would set up missiles along Soviet borders.
   - (D) He ordered an attack on the Soviet Union.

Lesson Objective (10–1:3)

9. Which of the following was a direct effect of Rosa Parks's refusal to give up her seat on a Montgomery bus?
   - (A) Freedom rides were organized to see if public transportation was obeying the law.
   - (B) Sit-ins were held at lunch counters and other public places across the South.
   - (C) Martin Luther King, Jr., helped organize a massive march in Washington, D.C.
   - ● Civil rights leaders organized a boycott on Montgomery buses.

Lesson Objective (10–1:4)

10. The Civil Rights Act of 1964
    - ● banned segregation in all public places.
    - (B) protected the rights of voters.
    - (C) made sit-ins and freedom rides illegal.
    - (D) outlawed segregation of the United States military.

Lesson Objective (10–2:1)

11. Who became the first American to orbit Earth?
    - (A) Yuri Gagarin
    - ● John Glenn
    - (C) Neil Armstrong
    - (D) Michael Collins

Lesson Objective (10–2:2)

12. What caused the United States to send troops to fight in Vietnam?
    - (A) Vietnamese soldiers who had fought for the French began moving north.
    - (B) Soviet and Chinese forces were trying to gain control of North Vietnam.
    - ● Ho Chi Minh's forces were winning the war against South Vietnam.
    - (D) The South Vietnamese were winning the war against the Viet Cong.

Lesson Objective (10–3:2)

13. Which of the following describes the National Organization for Women?
    - (A) an amendment that stated everyone must be treated exactly the same
    - ● an organization that worked toward equal opportunities for women
    - (C) an organization that used passive resistance to gain rights for migrant workers
    - (D) a law stating that federally funded public schools must offer equal opportunities to men and women

Lesson Objective (10–3:3)

14. Which of the following describes the Civil Liberties Act of 1988?
    - (A) ensures that no one is denied employment on the basis of race or sex
    - (B) makes it illegal to refuse to hire a qualified person because that person has a disability
    - ● apologized for the injustice endured by Japanese Americans during World War II
    - (D) rewarded Native Americans who served as code talkers during World War II

Lesson Objective (10–4:3)

15. Which of the following contributed to the collapse of communism in Europe?
    - ● The high cost of the arms race weakened the Soviet economy.
    - (B) Mikhail Gorbachev allowed less political and economic freedom than previous leaders.
    - (C) Cold War tensions increased between the United States and the Soviet Union.
    - (D) The Soviet Union refused to agree to an arms control agreement.

Part 2: Skills Test

Directions: Use complete sentences to answer questions 1–5. Use a separate sheet of paper if you need more space.

1. What was the main goal in forming the United Nations? **Summarize**

   World leaders had seen the devastation caused by war and wanted to work together to try to find peaceful solutions to international problems.

2. Complete the cause-and-effect chart below. Write an effect of the Voting Rights Act of 1965. **Cause and Effect**

   Cause: The Voting Rights Act of 1965 protected the rights of all Americans to vote.

   ↓

   Effect: **Many African Americans were able to vote for the first time.**

3. Identify two factors that made the Vietnam Conflict one of the most difficult wars ever fought by Americans. **Main Idea and Details**

   Much of the land was covered with mountains and thick jungles. North Vietnamese soldiers often used guerilla warfare tactics.

4. Suppose you wanted to find out what it was like to be a soldier in the Korean War. Do you think a primary or secondary source would be more helpful? Explain. **Compare Primary and Secondary Sources**

   Possible answer: A primary source such as a diary entry would be more helpful because it would offer a personal point of view.

5. Study the maps below. Which map would you use to compare the actual sizes of Greenland and South America? Explain. **Understand Map Projections**

   The equal-area projection map should be used because places that are closer to the poles appear larger than they really are on a Mercator projection.

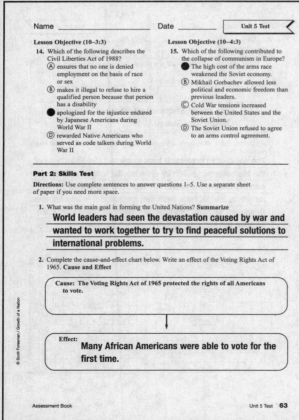

Equal-Area Projection

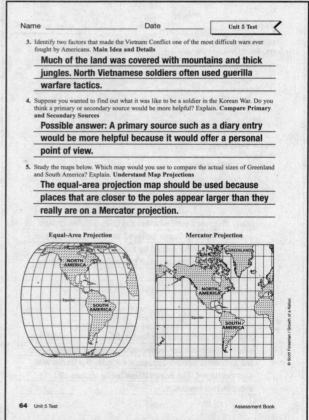

Mercator Projection

Chapter 11 Test

Part 1: Content Test

Directions: Fill in the circle next to the correct answer.

Lesson Objective (1:1)

1. Which region of the United States includes Kansas and Nebraska?
   - Ⓐ West
   - ● Midwest
   - Ⓒ Southwest
   - Ⓓ Southeast

Lesson Objective (1:2)

2. Which of the following describes a reason why the population of the Sunbelt increased rapidly?
   - Ⓐ Other regions were overcrowded and did not accept immigrants.
   - ● Many businesses moved there to take advantage of its natural resources.
   - Ⓒ Many workers moved there to take advantage of lower wages.
   - Ⓓ The invention of modern heating systems made it a more comfortable place to live.

Lesson Objective (1:3)

3. *E Pluribus Unum* means
   - ● "Out of many, one."
   - Ⓑ "I came, I saw, I conquered."
   - Ⓒ "For the people, by the people."
   - Ⓓ "Seize the day."

Lesson Objective (1:4)

4. Since the late 1900s, most immigrants have come from
   - Ⓐ Europe or Africa.
   - Ⓑ Europe or Asia.
   - ● Latin America or Asia.
   - Ⓓ Latin America or Africa.

Lesson Objective (2:1)

5. Which statement describes how the republican system of government works in the United States?
   - Ⓐ Each individual has the opportunity to vote on every decision the government makes.
   - Ⓑ The judicial branch makes the laws and the legislative branch runs the government.
   - ● Citizens elect representatives to make laws and run the government.
   - Ⓓ Citizens elect a President to make laws and run the government.

Lesson Objective (2:2)

6. Which of the following is NOT a responsibility of citizenship?
   - ● enforcing laws
   - Ⓑ paying taxes
   - Ⓒ serving on a jury
   - Ⓓ voting

Lesson Objective (2:2)

7. A 17-year-old citizen has all of the following basic rights EXCEPT
   - Ⓐ freedom of religion.
   - Ⓑ freedom of speech.
   - ● the right to vote.
   - Ⓓ the right to a fair trial.

Lesson Objective (2:3)

8. Which statement is true about the process for electing the President of the United States?
   - Ⓐ The number of electoral votes a candidate receives is based on the number of senators in each state.
   - Ⓑ Electors are appointed by the Supreme Court to determine who will become President.
   - Ⓒ It is possible for a candidate to win the electoral vote but still lose the election.
   - ● It is possible for a candidate to win a majority of the popular vote but still lose the election.

Lesson Objective (2:4)

9. Why is the Constitution called a living document?
   - Ⓐ Its authors are still living.
   - ● It can be changed over time.
   - Ⓒ It states that Supreme Court justices are appointed for life.
   - Ⓓ Only Supreme Court justices are allowed to add amendments.

Lesson Objective (3:1)

10. How does supply and demand affect businesses?
    - Ⓐ Consumers will only buy a product if the supply is high.
    - Ⓑ Supply and demand increases the opportunity cost of making a product.
    - Ⓒ Businesses can charge more if supply is high and demand is limited.
    - ● Businesses can charge more if supply is limited and demand is high.

Lesson Objective (3:2)

11. Which of the following had the greatest effect on the business and job markets in the late 1900s?
    - ● the computer
    - Ⓑ the invention of automobiles
    - Ⓒ the introduction of electricity
    - Ⓓ the aging population

Lesson Objective (3:3)

12. About what percentage of students between the ages of five and seventeen used computers in 2001?
    - Ⓐ 30 percent
    - Ⓑ 50 percent
    - Ⓒ 75 percent
    - ● 90 percent

Lesson Objective (3:4)

13. Which statement describes how the trading policies of the United States have changed in the late twentieth century?
    - Ⓐ The United States banned international trade.
    - ● The United States signed trade agreements with several countries.
    - Ⓒ The United States discouraged trade by placing higher tariffs on imports and exports.
    - Ⓓ The United States stopped trading with all countries except Canada and Mexico.

Lesson Objective (3:5)

14. Which of the following describes a result of globalization?
    - ● What happens to the economy in one country can affect the economy in other countries.
    - Ⓑ The system of free enterprise fails because competition no longer exists.
    - Ⓒ People and goods move less freely from one country to another.
    - Ⓓ The cultures of other countries become more isolated.

Lesson Objective (3:5)

15. Which of the following describes an effect of the interdependence between China and the United States after the Cold War?
    - Ⓐ The price of manufactured goods in the United States increased.
    - Ⓑ Many workers in China lost their jobs.
    - Ⓒ Companies and consumers in both countries suffered losses.
    - ● Companies and consumers in both countries profited.

Part 2: Skills Test

Directions: Use complete sentences to answer questions 1–5. Use a separate sheet of paper if you need more space.

1. Describe some effects of the growing diversity of immigrants that have come to the United States since the late 1900s. **Cause and Effect**

   The United States has a greater diversity of ethnic groups than ever before. The number of languages spoken and the variety of customs and religions has increased.

2. Complete the chart below. Summarize the details about the different ways to be an active citizen. **Summarize**

   | Detail: You can volunteer to help political candidates. | Detail: You can take part in a community project. | Detail: You can write or call political leaders to express your opinions. |

   Summary:

   Different ways to be an active citizen include volunteering for political candidates, participating in community projects, and expressing opinions to political leaders.

---

3. What is the North American Free Trade Agreement? **Summarize**

   It is an agreement that allows the United States, Canada, and Mexico to trade with each other without having to pay taxes or fees.

4. Suppose you want to find out more about the effects of globalization. Describe how you would use the Internet to research your topic. **Internet Research**

   Possible answer: Type "effects of globalization" in a search engine's search box. Click on the links to get more information on the topic. Choose Web sites that are reliable.

5. How would you use population density maps to compare two different regions of the United States? **Compare Population Density Maps**

   Possible answer: You could compare the population patterns in each region. For example, you might see if one region is more densely populated than the other region. You could also compare the population distribution of different areas in each region.

Chapter 12 Test

Part 1: Content Test

Directions: Fill in the circle next to the correct answer.

Lesson Objective (1:1)

1. Which of the following events occurred on September 11, 2001?
   - ● Terrorists crashed two planes into the twin towers of the World Trade Center.
   - Ⓑ Terrorists crashed two planes into the Pentagon.
   - Ⓒ Terrorists crashed a plane into the Capitol building.
   - Ⓓ Terrorists crashed a plane into the White House.

Lesson Objective (1:1)

2. About how many people were killed by the terrorist acts on September 11, 2001?
   - Ⓐ 1,500
   - ● 3,000
   - Ⓒ 5,000
   - Ⓓ 6,000

Lesson Objective (1:2)

3. Why are firefighters, police officers, and rescue workers remembered as heroes for their actions on September 11, 2001?
   - Ⓐ They collected toys and sent them to children who had lost loved ones.
   - Ⓑ They lined up to give blood to help those injured in the attacks.
   - ● They guided thousands of people to safety.
   - Ⓓ They delivered food and money to families in need.

Lesson Objective (1:3)

4. Why did the United States take military action against Afghanistan?
   - Ⓐ The Taliban organized the attacks of September 11, 2001.
   - ● The Taliban refused to capture Osama bin Laden and other al Qaeda leaders.
   - Ⓒ The Taliban carried out several attacks against American targets.
   - Ⓓ The Taliban opposed American influence in Western and Central Asia.

Lesson Objective (1:3)

5. Which event occurred in Afghanistan?
   - Ⓐ The United States captured Osama bin Laden and other al Qaeda leaders.
   - Ⓑ The Taliban captured Osama bin Laden and other al Qaeda leaders.
   - Ⓒ The United States worked with the Taliban to remove al Qaeda from power.
   - ● The Taliban was forced to surrender power.

Lesson Objective (1:3)

6. What happened when Saddam Hussein was again forced to admit weapons inspectors into Iraq?
   - ● Inspectors could not determine whether Iraq had weapons of mass destruction.
   - Ⓑ Inspectors found weapons that spread deadly diseases.
   - Ⓒ Inspectors found weapons that spread poison chemicals.
   - Ⓓ Inspectors found nuclear weapons.

Lesson Objective (1:3)

7. Why did American forces bomb Baghdad on March 20, 2003?
   - Ⓐ Iraq invaded Kuwait.
   - Ⓑ Iraq attacked the United States.
   - ● The United States wanted to remove Saddam Hussein from power.
   - Ⓓ Osama bin Laden was hiding in Baghdad.

Lesson Objective (2:1)

8. Which of the following might help protect the environment?
   - Ⓐ relying on nuclear power
   - Ⓑ burning more gasoline and coal
   - Ⓒ increasing the amount of carbon dioxide that is released in the atmosphere
   - ● decreasing the amount of carbon dioxide that is released in the atmosphere

Lesson Objective (2:1)

9. How might a car that runs on hydrogen fuel help protect the environment?
   - Ⓐ by releasing gases that would cool the global climate
   - ● by not producing air pollution
   - Ⓒ by eliminating the need for roads and highways
   - Ⓓ by releasing gases that would improve the atmosphere

Lesson Objective (2:2)

10. In 2000, about how many people in the world lived on less than $1 a day?
    - Ⓐ five thousand
    - Ⓑ one million
    - Ⓒ five million
    - ● one billion

Lesson Objective (2:2)

11. Where do most cases of malaria occur?
    - ● Africa
    - Ⓑ Australia
    - Ⓒ Europe
    - Ⓓ the United States

Lesson Objective (2:2)

12. What is Acquired Immunodeficiency Syndrome?
    - Ⓐ a disease that is caused by hunger
    - Ⓑ a disease that is caused by poverty
    - ● a disease that attacks people's immune systems
    - Ⓓ a disease that is spread by mosquitoes

Lesson Objective (2:2)

13. In what ways has Jimmy Carter worked to solve global problems?
    - ● by supporting free elections and helping to fight disease
    - Ⓑ by accepting the Nobel Peace Prize
    - Ⓒ by making a list of "Development Goals"
    - Ⓓ by developing medicines to fight malaria and AIDS

Lesson Objective (2:3)

14. What do scientists at the University of Southern California hope to use to help people with brain damage?
    - Ⓐ artificial intelligence
    - ● computer chips
    - Ⓒ jet airplanes
    - Ⓓ Martian rocks and soil

Lesson Objective (2:3)

15. What do scientists at NASA hope to develop by the year 2014?
    - Ⓐ satellites that can take pictures of Earth
    - Ⓑ a spacecraft that can orbit Earth
    - ● a spacecraft that can travel to Mars and bring samples back to Earth
    - Ⓓ a spacecraft that can travel to the moon

Part 2: Skills Test

Directions: Use complete sentences to answer questions 1–5. Use a separate sheet of paper if you need more space.

1. Read the passage. Write a sentence that is a generalization of the information in the passage. **Make Generalizations**

   > After the attacks of September 11, 2001, people all over the country lined up to give blood to help injured victims. Millions of people donated food, clothing, and money. Firefighters and other workers from cities and towns across the United States drove to New York City to help with the rescue effort.

   Following the attacks of September 11, Americans all over the country pulled together to face the challenges ahead.

2. What is al Qaeda and how has it affected the United States? **Main Idea and Details**

   Al Qaeda is a terrorist group headed by Osama bin Laden. The United States determined that al Qaeda planned the terrorist attacks of September 11, 2001. Al Qaeda also carried out several other attacks aimed at U.S. targets.

3. Why did some people support the use of military force against Iraq? Why did others believe that war was not necessary? **Compare and Contrast**

   Many believed that Saddam Hussein should be removed from power. They argued that he was a threat to his own people, neighboring countries, and the rest of the world. Others believed that United Nations inspectors should be given more time to determine whether Iraq possessed weapons of mass destruction.

---

4. What is global warming? Why are some scientists concerned about its effects? **Summarize**

   Global warming is the slow warming of the global climate caused by increased amounts of carbon dioxide in the atmosphere. Some scientists are concerned that this will cause environmental problems around the world.

5. Complete the chart below. Summarize the details about the global challenges people are working to solve. **Summarize**

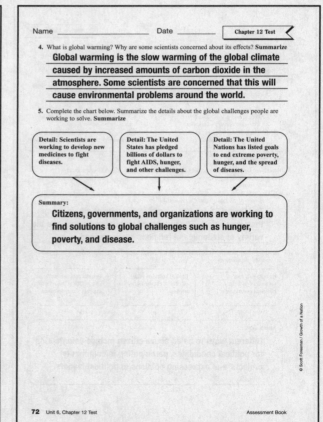

Detail: Scientists are working to develop new medicines to fight diseases.

Detail: The United States has pledged billions of dollars to fight AIDS, hunger, and other challenges.

Detail: The United Nations has listed goals to end extreme poverty, hunger, and the spread of diseases.

Summary: **Citizens, governments, and organizations are working to find solutions to global challenges such as hunger, poverty, and disease.**

Unit 6 Test

Part 1: Content Test

Directions: Fill in the circle next to the correct answer.

Lesson Objective (11–1:1)

1. In which region of the United States is California located?
   - Ⓐ Midwest
   - ● West
   - Ⓒ Southwest
   - Ⓓ Southeast

Lesson Objective (11–1:2)

2. Which of the following describes a reason why the population of the Sunbelt increased after World War II?
   - ● Many businesses came to take advantage of the warm climate, natural resources, and lower wages.
   - Ⓑ Many businesses came to take advantage of the warm climate, natural resources, and higher wages.
   - Ⓒ Many businesses came to take advantage of the cool climate, renewable resources, and lower wages.
   - Ⓓ Many businesses came to take advantage of the cool climate, natural resources, and higher wages.

Lesson Objective (11–1:4)

3. Where have most immigrants to the United States come from since the late 1900s?
   - Ⓐ Europe or Latin America
   - Ⓑ Europe or Africa
   - ● Asia or Latin America
   - Ⓓ Asia or Africa

Lesson Objective (11–2:1)

4. Which statement describes a republic?
   - ● People elect representatives to make laws and run the government.
   - Ⓑ People elect a President to make laws and run the government.
   - Ⓒ The President appoints representatives to make laws and run the government.
   - Ⓓ Each individual has the opportunity to vote on every decision the government makes.

Lesson Objective (11–2:2)

5. Responsibilities of citizenship include all of the following EXCEPT
   - Ⓐ obeying the law
   - Ⓑ serving on juries
   - Ⓒ paying taxes
   - ● making laws

Lesson Objective (11–2:3)

6. Which statement is true about the system that is used to elect the President of the United States?
   - Ⓐ The presidential candidate who gets a majority of the vote wins the election.
   - ● For most states, the presidential candidate who gets a majority of the vote in a state gets all of that state's electoral votes.
   - Ⓒ The two presidential candidates who get a majority of the vote are accepted to the electoral college.
   - Ⓓ Citizens in each city vote for electors to decide who will become President.

Lesson Objective (11–3:1)

7. How do consumers benefit from supply and demand?
   - Ⓐ If the supply and the demand are both high, prices will increase.
   - Ⓑ If the supply and the demand are both low, prices will increase.
   - ● If the supply is high and the demand is low, prices will decrease.
   - Ⓓ If the supply is low and the demand is high, prices will decrease.

Lesson Objective (11–3:2)

8. What became the two fastest-growing areas for jobs in the late 1900s and early 2000s?
   - Ⓐ education and social services
   - ● computers and health care
   - Ⓒ space technology and government
   - Ⓓ media and environmental science

Lesson Objective (11–3:4)

9. What is the purpose of the North American Free Trade Agreement?
   - Ⓐ to discourage trade between North American countries and the rest of the world
   - Ⓑ to encourage trade between North American countries and the rest of the world
   - Ⓒ to discourage trade between the United States, Canada, and Mexico
   - ● to encourage trade between the United States, Canada, and Mexico

Lesson Objective (12–1:1)

10. Which event did NOT occur on September 11, 2001?
    - Ⓐ Terrorists crashed two planes into the twin towers of the World Trade Center.
    - Ⓑ Terrorists crashed a plane into the Pentagon.
    - ● Terrorists crashed a plane into the White House.
    - Ⓓ A hijacked plane crashed in a field in Pennsylvania.

Lesson Objective (12–1:3)

11. Why did the United States attack Taliban troops and al Qaeda training bases in Afghanistan?
    - Ⓐ The Taliban and al Qaeda had carried out several attacks in the past against American targets.
    - Ⓑ The Taliban and al Qaeda claimed responsibility for the attacks of September 11.
    - Ⓒ Al Qaeda refused to capture Osama bin Laden and other Taliban leaders.
    - ● The Taliban refused to capture Osama bin Laden and other al Qaeda leaders.

Lesson Objective (12–1:3)

12. Why did the United States and Great Britain lead a coalition force into Iraq in 2003?
    - ● They wanted to remove Saddam Hussein from power.
    - Ⓑ They discovered weapons of mass destruction in Iraq.
    - Ⓒ Iraq invaded Kuwait and Saudi Arabia.
    - Ⓓ Osama bin Laden and other al Qaeda leaders were hiding in Iraq.

Lesson Objective (12–2:1)

13. Which of the following might help protect the environment in the future?
    - Ⓐ an increase in the use of coal
    - Ⓑ an increase of carbon dioxide
    - Ⓒ nuclear power
    - ● the hydrogen-fueled car

Lesson Objective (12–2:2)

14. About how many deaths does malaria cause each year?
    - Ⓐ one thousand
    - Ⓑ five thousand
    - ● two million
    - Ⓓ two billion

Lesson Objective (12–2:3)

15. What are scientists at NASA working to develop by the year 2014?
    - Ⓐ a machine with artificial intelligence
    - Ⓑ a computer chip to help people with brain damage
    - Ⓒ a satellite that can take pictures of Earth
    - ● a spacecraft that can travel to Mars and bring samples back to Earth

Part 2: Skills Test

Directions: Use complete sentences to answer questions 1–5. Use a separate sheet of paper if you need more space.

1. Read the passage. Write a sentence that is a generalization of the information in the passage. **Make Generalizations**

   > As a result of globalization, people today share more things than ever before. People all over the world can see the same movies and television shows, listen to the same music, and even dress alike. More and more people travel to foreign countries for both business and vacations.

   Globalization has had a great impact on cultures worldwide.

2. Describe how Americans responded to the terrorist attacks of September 11, 2001. **Main Idea and Details**

   Americans responded to the attacks with courage and caring. Emergency workers guided thousands of people to safety. Millions of people donated food, clothing, and money to victims of the attacks. People all over the country waited in lines to give blood to people injured in the attacks.

---

3. Complete the chart below. Summarize the details about the global challenges facing people around the world. **Summarize**

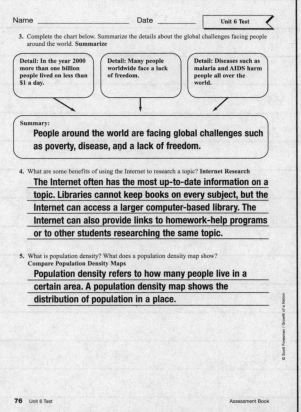

| Detail: In the year 2000 more than one billion people lived on less than $1 a day. | Detail: Many people worldwide face a lack of freedom. | Detail: Diseases such as malaria and AIDS harm people all over the world. |

Summary:
People around the world are facing global challenges such as poverty, disease, and a lack of freedom.

4. What are some benefits of using the Internet to research a topic? **Internet Research**

   The Internet often has the most up-to-date information on a topic. Libraries cannot keep books on every subject, but the Internet can access a larger computer-based library. The Internet can also provide links to homework-help programs or to other students researching the same topic.

5. What is population density? What does a population density map show? **Compare Population Density Maps**

   Population density refers to how many people live in a certain area. A population density map shows the distribution of population in a place.

NOTES

_____
_____
_____
_____
_____
_____
_____
_____
_____
_____
_____
_____
_____
_____
_____
_____
_____
_____
_____
_____
_____
_____
_____
_____

NOTES

NOTES

NOTES

NOTES

NOTES

NOTES

NOTES

NOTES